Red Wine

&

Cigarettes

Copyright © 2015 by Kathy D. Carter

ISBN-13: 978-0996374309
ISBN-10: 0996374302

All rights reserved worldwide. No part of this publication may be reproduced, stored in a retrieval system, or transmitted in any form orally or written or by any means, electronic, mechanical, recording or otherwise, without the prior written permission of the author.

Printed in

United States of America

Published by:

STF Publishing

Contact:

kathy@kathydcarter.com

Cover Art:

by Trent Ray

Model's photograph http://mejull.deviantart.com/

This book is for entertainment purposes and not intended as a substitute for the medical advice of physicians. The reader should regularly consult a physician in matters relating to his/her health and particularly with respect to any symptoms that may require diagnosis or medical attention.

Red Wine & Cigarettes

A self-help book on escaping thought seduction

and finding your one lost love.

by

Kathy D. Carter

DEDICATION

This book is dedicated to my two Children

Paul Rhymer & Bill Stiff

My Parents

My Sister

Jackie Glisson

My Doctors & Energy Healing Practitioners

My Warrior Spirit

The Universe

Without ALL of them and many others I would not be here to write my books!

Table of Contents

DEDICATION 4

INTRODUCTION 6

CHAPTER 1 - BELIEFS with Mr. Non-Judgmental 11

CHAPTER 2 - THOUGHTS with Mr. Exclusive 28

CHAPTER 3 - EMOTIONS with Mr. Renaissance 37

CHAPTER 4 - HUMAN BODY with Mr. Geronimo 52

CHAPTER 5 - TOOLS with Mr. Backup 63

CHAPTER 6 - FOOD FOR THOUGHT with Mr. Wonder 84

CHAPTER 7 - MY STORY with Mr. Columbian 99

INTRODUCTION

I had a man say he had been bad in his previous life and they sent him to Earth. I like to think that I too was bad and sent here to Earth to meet up with him. We have a mission buried within us to change the world. He wants to fight it out, and I want to love it out. That's where the contrast of Earth starts. The yin and yang, the black and white, the high and the low, the stilettos and the oxfords, the good and the bad, the light and the dark, the frozen and the hot, the closed and the free, the soft and the rough, and the slow and the fast are all examples of contrast. Without contrast we would never fully enjoy anything. We can find something good in everything that happens or exists.

I'm evolving and what I believe and say today may change tomorrow, except maybe for the next statement. If you have a pain, heal the emotion-thought-belief connected to it and it will be gone. So by the time you read this I will have evolved and may or may not still believe everything I write here today. However, I will not let that be a rationalization or excuse for not sharing what I have learned so far on my path and what has helped me so much in my growth.

I was called a "science fiction person" just yesterday by someone who found my thoughts unbelievable and strange to him. We are each at our own level of vibrational frequency as I call it and this book will seem like science fiction to some people, old news to others, and all degrees of helpfulness to many others. The many others are the ones I'm hoping to help, if only with one of my suggestions or thoughts in this book. However, my belief is that if this book is before you right now, there is something in it for you that can change your life.

The old cliché....This book may not be for you, but if it's already in your hands and you've read this much, then I ask you to be open and just listen to my viewpoints. They may sound very absurd to you and may make you very angry and upset or you may agree and smile.

Your emotions are your body's GIFT to say that you have a belief that differs with mine. That's all!

My purpose of this book is to get people to *FEEL* their emotions and uncover the beliefs (conscious or unconscious) that are causing those emotions.

Beliefs cause thoughts which in turn cause emotions. Control *your* brain. Use your brain. Don't give your brain the control panel and ability to use you. Take responsibility for what your life is. You create your life with your thoughts! You create your life with how you treat yourself.

Lots of authors have already said this. I'm just saying it again hoping to help those of you who still want more explanation. Like me....I know you have heard we teach what we are trying to learn ourselves. We really do create our life with our thoughts. So it only follows that you can change your life! Just uncover your beliefs, examine them, and maybe decide you want some NEW beliefs to live by.

Now let me tell you a little more about my style of teaching. Please excuse my sometimes harsh and direct to the point communication. I am an Aries. I am different, I don't follow all the rules and I blaze my own way. It is who I am and I'm proud of it finally. I am working on being a softer, sweeter, sexier and stronger person. However, that hasn't been completely manifested by me in my life at this point but I'm still working on it. I can say I am a surviving Warrior.

I am not saying or doing anything new. I am just presenting it in a different way. Hopefully for a fuller meaningful understanding for those who still want or need help. I hope to make it easier to grasp and give you tools to implement easier quicker change in your life. For instance using the Quippet can really help. All you have to do to heal is to stay in a higher vibration. Notice first of all when you are in a low vibration then immediately step in and raise it. Control your Thoughts, Control your Brain. The Brain is your computer and you control and supply the software input. Damaged Negative Beliefs result in Damaged Negative Thoughts that result in Negative Emotions that are low vibration such as fear and anger. Do a Quippet and see what is right in this moment.

I see the big picture. I state things how I see them with as few words and as simple as I can. I suggest ways of healing that worked for me. There are as many ways to heal as there are different religions, brands of toothpaste, kinds of alcoholic drinks, choices of chocolate desserts and kinds of breakfast cereals. So it is *necessary* to pick your path and stick to it.

I suggest that you not go on a continual life shopping spree of healing methods because that's addictive and is truly an avoidance technique of healing and doing your work. So is continuing to complain of the pain when in fact it is gone and you just won't release that idea because it scares you to take responsibility for yourself. So your choice on *that* road is to become what I call a "professional patient of whatever illness you claim"……be it professional heart disease patient, professional cancer patient, or professional environmental illness patient.

You become the expert professional of all the causes and ways to protect yourself and possibly you become a "respected" resource person by fellow ill people but you never recover because it scares you to finish healing and be who you really are. Of course, there is always the possibility that is the life contract you signed up for. I never have the intent to intentionally hurt anyone or be mean or lack tact with someone. I apologize if that happens. The intent of this book is to shake up and wake up your rote repeated thinking patterns and that needs some direct strong language sometimes.

Also remember anytime something you read or something someone says to you pushes your buttons (causes an emotional response), forget the person or author and go DIRECTLY to the feeling by identifying your emotion, thoughts and beliefs causing it. **That is your work** and my job with this book is to help you really learn how to do that. I want you to make it a reflex action when you *feel* an emotion.

CHAPTER 1 - BELIEFS with Mr. Non-Judgmental

Tell me your fantasies Mr. Non-Judgmental, a Scorpio, said. I'm the most non-judgmental person you will ever meet and he was! He was so open and honest. He was considerate, sincere and caring. He seemed to always be in the present moment drinking in all the details of the surroundings as well as the action taking place. He remembered them all. He appeared to me to have all the good characteristics that Christian Grey had.

I was taken aback by his request. After all, I'd never shared my fantasies with anyone not even my previous husbands. He saw my reserve and said think about it because I want to hear them. You are probably curious how this friendship started. Well, we met through a dating site. Now that brings up a stigma for many people. They are very hesitant to say we met on a dating site. I think it's time we get over that because lots of people meet that way now. It's a change and people resist change. I wanted him to call again but when I didn't hear from him I let him go from my mind. I have beliefs I still haven't changed that keep me from being the first to make contact with a male.

On a Saturday around 1:00 p.m. a couple of weeks later, much to my surprise, he sent a message asking if I could meet him a few hours later that very day. I'm very spontaneous and loved his approach, still with the thought that's really quick notice. I was working so I asked if a couple hours later would be ok and he agreed. We met and had a fantastic time. We played some pool which of course he was a pro at but didn't tell me until a later time. He was having fun watching me try to play. He allowed me to have fun and some competition without clearing the table on his first turn. He was good at a lot of things and he had lived life to the fullest. If he wanted to do something he did it or made plans to do it. We met the following day and continued to date 2-3 times a week for awhile.

He was taller than me but not of a big build yet I felt very protected and safe in his arms. He had very distinctive six pack abs which he said he came by naturally with little exercise and he was very muscular. His body was impressive. He was very athletic and enjoyed playing soccer, watching Formula One car racing, deep sea fishing, and any and all activities that provided him with the thrill of living life. He enjoyed life to the fullest. I really wanted to know a lot more about this man.

We always had very deep philosophical conversations which I enjoyed immensely. We would be sitting talking and he would rest his elbows on his knees and lean in to me asking some deep question or making a very deep statement to study and record my reaction in his memory. He was always mixing drinks for me and asking what I liked or didn't like and then adjusting the next drink accordingly. He would say you liked that and you'll love this. He was so calm, cool, sexy and collected always looking at me and seeing deep inside my soul like no other man had ever done. He watched me cook, walk and talk. He studied me intensely.

We would be deep in philosophical conversation for hours at a time. Time flies when you are matched with someone on all levels. All the sudden he would move into my space even closer, so intriguing and so romantic. He was so soft and easy and giving of love and support. Yet he was also domineering and I was unable to resist him. Nor did I even want to resist his commanding gaze and touch. He'd kiss me softly on the neck in the spot where no man ever finds causing me to melt with his touch. Then after what seemed like hours, still in deep conversation he would stand and hold out his hand wanting mine. He would lead me upstairs to the bedroom. He was so gentle and understanding yet was such a commanding force. He was so open and vulnerable letting me know how he felt about certain touches that he'd never experienced with any other woman and how wonderful it felt. I was amazed at his level of communication about his emotions and his openness. I had never been with a man like that before.

He stated a few times that he was tired of life on Earth and was ready to leave. My response was always that you need to know that it is your time because they won't let you go if it's not. I had tried and they wouldn't let me go. I also suggested that if that was really the case he needed to make sure he did it right. I didn't want to see him laid up paralyzed or something for the rest of his life. He told me he couldn't stay here with all the pain and disruption that was occurring on Earth. He never fully explained to me his theory of cause and effect of life that he lived by, because he said he had really upset and disturbed other people with it and would not do that to me. I was curious to know and understand it, but he never explained it to me.

About three months into the relationship, I was to meet him and he asked if we could move it to the next day. I said of course. The next day I was in his neighborhood working and text him about our evening a few times and never got a response back. I told him I was going on home to wait to hear from him. My gut didn't feel right. I waited a day and sent another text wishing him the best in life and that I had really enjoyed our time together. I had concluded with my brain software that he had moved on and I needed to let him go even though that didn't feel right to me. How could that be? He had told me his door was open any hour of the day or night for me.

Well during the next six weeks or so, my brain went on all kinds of output and deductive reasoning. He was a no good son of a gun for not even explaining anything to me. I asked myself so many times what had I done to turn him away like that. I went through every emotion and thought possible in those six weeks. I knew none of his friends and he knew none of mine. Our times together had always been alone and very deep into discovering who each other was. I googled his name within the first few weeks several times with no results and gave up. I had to accept what had happened. He had moved on and I needed to also. I am so very grateful for our precious time together. He taught me so much in such a very short time.

This story and everything I learned with Mr. Non-Judgmental leads me into the discussion of beliefs we hold within ourselves. Please read the following list of beliefs and notice what your thoughts are.

List of a few beliefs:

- ❖ Scientist's thoughts alter and have an affect/effect on their experiment's results.
- ❖ Flowers can sing.
- ❖ Trees can cry.
- ❖ I trust life.
- ❖ I am safe.
- ❖ Humans can regrow severed limbs.

- ❖ You grow younger looking as you clear energy blockages.
- ❖ Wrinkles disappear as you release old stored traumas.
- ❖ You can grow younger and feel more youthful.
- ❖ We can live healthy and physically active for as long as we want to.
- ❖ We can transition (die) without suffering, illness and decline.
- ❖ We find what we look for.
- ❖ We all talk telepathically on the highways or there would be millions of accidents daily.
- ❖ Acidic water is proven to be a very effective sanitizer and disinfectant.
- ❖ We must use toxic cleaners to sterilize our hospitals and nursing homes and public places.
- ❖ More is always better.
- ❖ I have no control over the situation.
- ❖ I will always be poor.
- ❖ Money is hard to come by.
- ❖ Money is the root of all evil.
- ❖ Life is a struggle.
- ❖ There is nothing I can do.
- ❖ That is just the way it is.
- ❖ That is the way it has always been.
- ❖ I've always done it this way.
- ❖ Things never change.
- ❖ I cannot change.
- ❖ We will never know.
- ❖ I don't know.
- ❖ I forget.
- ❖ I didn't see.
- ❖ Good, righteous, God faring people suffer and struggle to survive.
- ❖ The more we suffer and struggle the better person we are.
- ❖ Evil, bad people have lots of money and they got it by wrong means.
- ❖ Everyone that has lots of money got it the wrong way.

- ❖ I'm more worthy if I have to suffer and struggle and work very hard.
- ❖ The more I suffer and struggle and work very hard the more worthy I become.
- ❖ If I'm worthy (suffer, struggle and work very hard) then I will be valued and loved and wanted.
- ❖ If a person never calls me again I did something to force them away.
- ❖ I don't deserve good things because I am unlikeable.

Now I would like for you to take a moment and think about the thoughts that came to you as you read this list. If you have forgotten, then please reread the list and try to catch your thoughts in response to each one. Most likely you agreed or strongly disagreed with each one, or it made you curious about it whether you believed the statement or not. You experienced a lot of emotion when you read these. I hope you were able to identify, and most of all, feel those emotions.

For example when you read that humans could regrow severed limbs I'm sure you had a reaction. Many of you began to agree with the man that called me a science fiction person. Some of you may have thrown down the book saying this is totally absurd and she really is crazy! Yet some of you may have wondered if that is really possible. This is the point I'm trying to make. We are looking through our own special filters. The thoughts you had and the emotions you felt were all formed and coming from the beliefs that you hold as true.

Do we really gain weight or gain body fat because of the food consumed or more because of our self-defeating beliefs? I can put on five pounds just looking at food. I cannot lose weight. Why do people die of starvation when others live only on air and water or very little to thrive on? Do we need protein to build muscle? Or do we need the belief our body is a magnificent machine and will build muscle from anything we give it, because it adapts expertly.

Beliefs can be broken down into many categories such as conscious and unconscious and collective conscious and collective unconscious and so on. I am all about the big picture and the big picture on this issue is that our beliefs control our thoughts which in turn control our emotions and our emotions control our lives. So in a nutshell our beliefs control our life! I challenge you to examine your beliefs and understand what you really do believe. I challenge you to excavate your unconscious beliefs and bring them to consciousness. At least "know" what is controlling your brain.

You are unaware of your unconscious beliefs but also unaware of your so well rutted beliefs. If you sit still and set your intent that you want to know them, your inner healer now goes to work. By the way, your inner healer is now jumping with joy that you have decided to work in union with her or him. When you work with your inner healer, your body, and your emotions, you start to gain control of your motherboard – your brain!

Help and information do come when you ask for it. Set your intent every morning for the day. Also set your intent for everything you do. It works wonders. You will love the way things start turning out differently. It's so easy, but you have to remain in the present moment in order to do this successfully. Retrain your brain. Take control of your thoughts. Examine and change your beliefs that need it.

This brings us to people who are labeled open minded and people who are labeled as closed minded. Closed minded people in my opinion have such deep brain ruts that a car could never be found if driven off into that rut. It is very hard for these people to change, but it can be done. A common statement they will say is I have always done it this way or that's the way it is.

I do have tremendous compassion for them and especially for those who chose to change those deep brain ruts. It is hard challenging work but so rewarding. I have been there and succeeded in excavating and changing some of my buried close minded unconscious beliefs. I admit that I still have much more to do. It truly is all about enjoying the journey. We never get it all done.

For example let me tell you about one particular belief I excavated and saw how it was controlling my life. Upon asking and much soul searching I discovered that if I did something wrong I believed it was a sin. I also uncovered that I believed if I made a mistake it was also a sin. I believed if I committed a sin I would go to hell and burn forever.

I therefore uncovered that every time I did something wrong I had committed a sin, was a sinner, and would burn in hell forever. I was not feeling very good about myself nor did I want to do much decision making for fear of doing it wrong and being a greater sinner and building a bigger fire. A family member always said he didn't want to be cremated because he didn't want to start the fire for them. This belief kept me paralyzed without me really knowing what was going on because it was an unconscious belief that controlled my life. I didn't want to venture out and challenge myself or try walking through any fears, because the fears already in me had me paralyzed. I thought it best to just keep a low profile and try not to make a mistake.

I also uncovered that I believed and had been taught that I was responsible for how everyone else felt. If they were unhappy it was my fault. Whatever emotion they felt I was the cause of it and responsible for their not feeling happy. I grew up in a very depressed and therefore very unhappy negative area of the country. I carried a very heavy burden upon myself feeling so responsible at a very early age in life. But the saving grace of this belief was that I was never responsible for how I felt; it was somebody else's action that made me feel that way. The ways we get so screwed up!

This belief caused me to be labeled a "people pleaser" and for good reason. Damn, if I was responsible for all these people, I was going to try and please them to give them at least a little ray of happiness or smile every now and then if at all possible. That way I could feel a little happiness for myself by doing something right and being wanted by them. Although, I always felt afterwards that I could have done it better. The perfectionist in me was showing up. That however is another story for another time. Oh, wow, overcoming the perfectionist in us! There are endless tendrils woven in us to unravel from the perfectionist standpoint.

So as the people pleaser I wanted and did everything everybody asked me to do. I couldn't displease anyone. That would be wrong and therefore a sin. So I did things I didn't really want to do or have time to do. But I became a pro at being a people pleaser. I'd bake the cookies for the bake sale. I'd get the house cleaned for entertaining as well as work all day and cook and serve the food to the guests that night. I'd accomplish the work of three people in the office. I was an excellent organizer and accomplished in one day more than 2 or 3 non-perfectionist people pleasing people could have done in a week. However, I found myself overworked, tired, and a little resentful on the inside of myself. I noticed the resentment and dissatisfaction was growing with the years. But I was able to portray the perfect female on the outside. The following quotes sum it up.

I could "bring home the bacon, fry it up in a pan, and never ever let you forget you're a man" "/Enjoli commercial (1980s)

> Peggy Lee (1963) "I can scoop up a great big dipper full of lard from the drippins can
>
> Throw it in the skillet, go out & do my shopping, be back before it melts in the pan
>
> 'Cause I'm a woman! W-O-M-A-N, I'll say it again"

It is also like the female with past society programming that wants to feel sexy and wear a garter belt and hose, wear lacy gloves, high heels, sexy lingerie, pretty makeup, role play, wear clothes others say are not age appropriate, wear a shorter skirt, wear a deep slit in her skirt, wear a special hat, get a new hairdo, but won't because she believes it is sinful, wrong, makes her a whore, makes her a slut, makes her too aggressive, means she is bad, or some other excuse and or belief that comes up to keep her under control. She is not enjoying her sexuality and life as she really wants to. That is when the resentment and dissatisfaction starts growing. You are not being true to yourself and your desires. I say that we say No to all the past programming and follow our hearts and our own internal moral compass. I won't play the belief controlled victim anymore, and I ask you to question yourself if you still want to play that person.

I believe that women as a whole have a hard time being open and honest when it comes to their sexuality. Mr. Wonder and I just discussed this the other day. He was saying that most women will not talk openly about what they like and want sexually. He said a lot of them shut down when he brings up the subject. I believe this is unconscious behavior on their part and comes largely from the collective unconscious of the many years women have been oppressed, owned as property and controlled. Women are ingenious and they learned how to manipulate and lie in order to survive. Today most women are still trying to liberate from the old ways and become more open and honest.

When I ask a female why she won't buy herself that skirt or hat or garter belt, she immediately clarifies while blushing or getting angry and very defensive that she could never do that. She is not that kind of woman. I beg her to explore what beliefs she is running about "that kind of woman". Is it a woman that is free to feel and play with her sexuality and desires? I don't think so.

Close minded people have "immediate" unconscious denial-resistance responses to comments or situations. These people are most likely very unconscious of what they are really saying. If a statement is made to them like you are trying to control people their IMMEDIATE words are No, I do not control people, when in fact they are experts at controlling others. It is no wonder we don't feel good when we are living such paradoxes in our lives. Watch what is happening when you get defensive.

Here is another example of how beliefs control us. A friend of mine was complaining about all the typing needed to text and I asked her why she didn't use the microphone feature of her phone. She replied she couldn't use it because she would have to download software followed with more excuses. I said I don't think so. All you have to do is hit the picture of the microphone and speak. It will do the typing. It's that quick and easy.

Being the person she was, she still didn't believe me and didn't try it right then. However, she is an open-minded, intelligent, curious individual and a few days later thanked me. She told me how much easier it was to use the microphone, and no she didn't have to do anything else. There was no software to download or anything else to do. She just had to push the microphone button and talk. Yet she had believed there was and had not even tried. We are birds just sitting "trapped" in an open door cage. We don't see that we can just fly out the open door and be free to be ourselves.

Repeating the same phrases or actions over and over results in repeating patterns in the brain. I call these brain ruts. The definition of a rut is a sunken track or groove made by the passage of vehicles especially on dirt roads. A brain rut is something our brain performs without hesitation or us having to instruct it to do so. That is partly why we aren't aware of our beliefs because they are buried in the brain ruts. We are on autopilot.

A good brain rut is pulling our hand away quickly from a hot flame or getting on a bike and riding it or driving a car providing we have already learned this. A bad brain rut or road block to what we want is the belief there is not enough time, or not enough money, or I don't have enough education, or I'm not good enough. These statements and rationale run so automatically in our brain that we are not even aware of thinking them. They are also victim statements.

Try this experiment for me. The next time you say "I can't" replace those words with "I won't". This helps place the responsibility on you for making the choice of I won't, instead of saying I can't which makes you feel relieved of responsibility for the action. Another way of looking at this is that saying can't is playing a victim. Be a creator and say I won't. Try to make this a daily practice forevermore of always replacing I can't with I won't. It will help you discover more information about who you really are and what choices you are really making.

Let's explore the filters through which we see our life. Our filters are actually our beliefs. Everyone has filters and some have cloudier lenses than others. If a person driving their car cuts you off and blows their horn at you, what reaction would you have? What thoughts run through your brain? One person might immediately get angry, their blood pressure increases, and they blow their horn back at the person and try to cut them off. Another submissive person might smile and quickly let them in.

Please remember that everything is relative to the situation. What I am about to discuss could take a book to explain. I am just trying to explain what I mean by the filters through which we see life. The first person's defensive reaction of retaliation is probably coming from cloudy life filter lenses. This may be a person that has stored anger in their energy field that is unresolved and is creating a blockage. Something about the incident "triggered" an extremely old memory that they have buried and forgotten about except that it is still controlling their life. The old memory contains a lot of unreleased anger.

The second person's reaction could also be coming from cloudy filter lenses. This person was also triggered by an old stored memory that causes them to go passive and not stand up for themselves; and then they act like the most perfect polite understanding person that lives. I can sense the fakeness that radiates in their response. This person is also a time bomb waiting to explode. They too have stored anger in their energy field that is unresolved and is creating a blockage.

Our "story of our history" that we tell controls our lives. It can create several more cloudy layers on our life filter lenses or it can remove some layers. It all depends on how you tell your "story". I want you to become acutely aware of how you tell your stories. Better yet, stop telling PAST history stories of your life altogether! Only tell future imagined happy ending stories of how you want your life!

For example, I almost drowned once in the eighth grade. I had a girl on my shoulders who was really short and couldn't swim. I was pulled deeper into the water until my head was under and I no longer had control of us. She panicked and wouldn't let me pull her off my shoulders so I could come up for air.

She had been loud previously, so when she started screaming trying to get help for us no one really listened for awhile. I knew not to take water into my lungs, I knew I couldn't get her off my shoulders, and I remember deciding to concentrate on just holding my breath. I remember coming to being drug out of the water by two older high school guys. We were in about ankle deep water by this time and I started coughing. I became embarrassed at this point and said I was ok when in reality I wasn't and they knew it. They continued to help me to shore. I remember this incident like it occurred in slow motion.

Now I have choices about how I tell this story. I could have told this story about how I nearly drowned in the eighth grade and how frightened I am of the water. I will never get in water again because of that incident. I could tell this story with lots of drama, sympathy and attention seeking statements. I think you understand. I could be the victim of the incident and story. I could have let this incident control the rest of my life in a way of never swimming again. However, I usually tell it just like I did above. Recently, I fully enjoyed many hours of being out in a kayak in the Pacific Ocean.

Let's read some more beliefs.

- Everything is relative.
- Anything in excess is bad.
- Sex is sinful.
- Real men do not cry.
- A woman needs a man in order to survive. She cannot make it on her own.
- A woman must serve her man.
- A man must serve his woman.
- We must stay together for the kids.
- Marriage is forever.
- Do something wrong and it is a sin.
- Commit a sin and you will go to hell and burn forever.
- Who created the right and wrongs?
- You must teach a child by hitting them. It is the only way they will learn.
- She is pregnant and you must marry her.
- Older women should not wear short skirts or sexy clothes.
- Those clothes are not age appropriate.
- Ice melts. Maybe ice melts, it is relative to the temperature.
- You cannot wear white shoes or white pants after Labor Day.
- TV commercials program your brain's software with your permission.
- It is okay that I may die as a side effect from taking this prescribed medication.
- If I use this toothpaste, cologne, perfume, or wear these sunglasses, I will attract a loving partner.
- More is better.

So I gave you another small list of beliefs to think about and do your work on. Did you feel it, catch it, and excavate it? Just reading beliefs can cause your thoughts that cause your emotions. See how it works?

What is addiction? I define addiction as a brain rut. Usually the body at some point needed to store or wall away some event that the person could not handle at the age it happened, or it was just so traumatic the person wasn't age appropriate on knowing how to handle it, or it was just so blatantly traumatic the body had to wall it off to survive. We find addictions to avoid ever having to heal that event.

The body being the self-healing machine that it is tries to maintain homeostasis. It gives us warning signals that something isn't balanced and right. We may have a slight pain, some anxiety, a need to flee or run, a very uncomfortable feeling, an unexpected strong anger response or some other feeling or emotion as it tries to heal a stored experience. These warning signals usually come in a neutral situation but we go into drama not understanding what is really happening. I believe we need to teach our children what emotions are and how to work with them to heal themselves.

At this point in a situation of feeling something really uncomfortable and not understanding it, it is easier to "stuff" that feeling or emotion by eating food, drinking alcohol, helping others, following Facebook, being on your phone, having sex, shopping, exercising, working, taking legal drugs, taking illegal drugs or anything else to excess or at least to the point that we numb the feeling we were having.

These activities give us a high, and feel better than the warning signal our body was giving us to help us heal. We chose to ignore our body's wisdom and seek the instant gratification and stuff further down in our body what needs healed. It would be much healthier to recognize and deal with what our body is trying to tell us. Something stored in the body is easier to take care of the quicker it receives your attention. The longer it remains stored, the more energy it requires to release and heal it.

When we get quiet our body tries to let us know what needs healed. I believe this is the main reason most people do not want to meditate or be alone or be quiet because this is when the body starts sending items up to consciousness to be healed so it can keep the body healthy. We are not taught this belief or the tools to understand how to deal with what is happening in the body. We have become so proficient at not listening to our bodies, and not wanting to feel uncomfortable, and not wanting to visit something unknown. We have an Inner Healer that we need to become acquainted with and listen to, in order to preserve good health. Our bodies are so much more complex, advanced, and sophisticated than we realize and appreciate.

When we do activities to excess to stuff our feelings or emotions, we have decidedly shut down our body's communication with us that something is amiss. Most of us take better care of our cars than we do our bodies. If the engine light comes on or the car doesn't run right, we get it into the garage as soon as possible to see what is wrong. Yet when our body is not running smoothly, we have been taught to push on and work through it. Most of us pay more attention to the physical and emotional needs of our children, friends and strangers than we do to our own bodies.

Our emotions are the same to our body as the engine light is to your car. Start noticing your emotions and your body will run and feel much better.

If we are tired, most of us will not sit down and rest. If we are thirsty, most of us wait to get a drink. If we are hungry, most of us do not sit down and enjoy eating our food. We eat it on the run, like our body doesn't deserve the right to enjoy the food. If we are sick, we do not usually take off work and rest. That house dust, that letter that needs written, those dishes that need washed, and that errand that needs run, will all still be there later. This is not advocating addiction to procrastination or using the situation to "control" others.

We have been taught to ignore our body's magnificent warning system which is our emotions and symptoms that our body gives us! We have been told we are weak and not strong if we don't keep going. We must work hard and suffer a lot to be a good person. I am saying I do not believe this anymore!

I do not know of any company that paid an employee extra for never taking their breaks. However I know of MANY employees that do not take their breaks, that are granted by law, and yet they complain of being overworked. We overachieve in an attempt to be accepted and needed from an outside source, when in reality we need to be loving and accepting ourselves internally. Complaining of being overworked is the victim mentality. It is also living our life from a foundation of unknown beliefs. Our brain has the control of our life. We are not in control of our very own brain; we are operating in runaway autopilot mode.

CHAPTER 2 - THOUGHTS with Mr. Exclusive

Wear a button down the front blouse with a shelf bra, wear a skirt that unzips, wear thigh highs, and sexy underwear says Mr. Exclusive, a Capricorn man. He also says not to wear a lot of makeup, because he doesn't like a lot of makeup on a woman. He tells me to wear high heels. The rest of what I wear, he leaves for me to decide. I am to meet him at a predestined place at a certain time and not be late. He liked the black velvet choker I chose to wear that first night.

He opened the door and pulled me inside. He kissed me long and meaningful on the lips before moving to that very tantalizing spot that I possess on the back of my neck which he didn't know about. He zoned in on that spot intuitively like he did a lot of moves. This all happened and much more, before any words were spoken out loud. Much communication was going on without speaking.

Mr. Exclusive made love with me. We did not have just sex. There is a difference between having sex and making love. I was able to connect on a deep level with him and reach orgasm over and over. More than I ever had before. He put all his attention and focus on unbuttoning my blouse. He handled each button seductively in a demanding open eye gaze all the time, and demanding that my eyes stay open and focused on his eyes. I felt him penetrating me with every button he opened. He slowly and intentionally removed my blouse, before moving to more kissing all over my body. He stood back looking at my body and admiring every inch of it.

I was craving and wanting him to take me all the more but he had the control. He was persistent and demanded the same from me. It was some of the most beautiful sensuous love making sessions I've ever had. His body was like Mr. Non-Judgmental and very close to being like Mr. Geronimo's body. He was toned, muscular and in the best shape of any man I'd ever had the privilege of touching and being with. Every date with Mr. Exclusive was an excellent anticipated event and one of the most open-hearted loving experiences I've ever had.

Mr. Exclusive and I had discussed all of our likes and dislikes openly and candidly before ever meeting the first time. He was the first man I had ever done this with. He would ask anything and I would have to answer him. It was liberating. I learned so many things about myself, that he taught me and prompted me to examine and reconsider.

I studied my connotations to words and my unspoken beliefs that were programmed into me. It is the intention that words are spoken with that matters. Intention is the energy and feeling and emotion with which the words are spoken. Being called a slut or whore can be so romantic and loving and fun for both partners, when it is accepted as such by both partners and they have examined and changed their beliefs. I'll bet that statement made some emotions. He was my introduction to the dominant and submissive world of love making. It was so intriguing and lots of fun. I learned so much about letting go and trusting another. He wanted to buy me a beautiful collar to wear everyday and be available at his call. I could not find it within myself to agree to that.

I could have told Mr. Exclusive no, and not have discussed anything with him; however, I would have missed learning so very much about myself and my beliefs. He was a good teacher and provoker for me. He would not let me avoid anything. He helped me become more open and honest with myself and others. He was a lot like Mr. Match in that way.

Our thoughts create our life, and generally for most people their thoughts are on auto play. An undirected brain on the loose creates repeating runaway garbage thoughts. Your thoughts are created from your software, that you have let someone else program. Is that really how you want your life to be created? Would you think that maybe you are playing victim here, and letting someone else control your life for you?

The Victim personality has beliefs like I have to work hard to get ahead, I'm not good enough, I don't have enough money, the harder I work and more I suffer the better person I am, something is wrong with me. The victim has many statements of fear. The victim really has fear of how great they could be if they stepped up and really took responsibility for their own lives and left everyone else alone.

The Creator personality has beliefs like everything I need will be provided, I am loved, I am needed, I will do well to be a good example for others, I am worthy of having what I desire, I am grateful for my life, and I have a special purpose to fulfill here. The Creator takes charge of their life, and looks at every experience in it as a growing and learning experience. They determine how best to handle whatever situation arises in front of them in their life. They do not choose to run on autopilot.

Are you a Victim of your illness or are you a Creator using your illness for growth and change in your life? The victim claims to not be able to help what is happening to them and then use the illness as a subtle tool to control everyone around them. Do you want to change your life? I've told you how and will explain it more later on. You can institute change without going as far as creating an illness in your body to get your attention. Pay attention to your emotions and constantly work at raising them to a higher vibrational frequency. That is all you have to do! Do a Quippet!

Examine your thoughts and beliefs that are coming up about why this won't work!!! Be the Creator of your life and take responsibility. Quit giving away your power. Walk through the FEAR of being all you can be……

Or you can choose to be a Victim and do the following.

- believe it is okay that death is an acceptable side effect of your prescribed medication
- Let someone else claim your power and program the software of your brain
- Continue to be a Victim, and claim life is treating you badly
- be powerless
- be taken care of
- suffer
- be less than you are
- refuse to complete your Earthly contract you signed up for
- control everyone around you, instead of controlling yourself
- complain all the time, be grumpy
- fault finding, making yourself always right
- take prescription drugs unnecessarily
- see what's wrong in the moment
- get sympathy
- regardless of how, get more attention
- stay little

- stay less than
- be the worse
- suffer the most, talk about how bad you have it
- be a bitch
- frown a lot

This is easier to do than being a Creator and taking responsibility for your life. Why not be a Creator of your life and see what is right in every moment.

- ask what the illness is here to teach you
- ask what can I learn from this pain
- know your body can heal itself
- learn to breathe correctly
- learn to be present, relax, meditate
- learn to listen to your intuition
- quit ignoring, and believe in and practice your gifts
- believe you will be supplied with everything you need
- believe there is abundance of everything including time, money, and love
- excavate your unknown beliefs and transform them
- learn to manage your body's energy
- learn to control your brain
- use your brain instead of letting it have control over you by just running in its old ruts
- truly love and forgive yourself
- believe in the impossible
- believe in miracles
- let go of the rationalization and avoidance statement that this is all Pollyanna thinking
- know we can be whatever we truly want to be
- smile, and smile again
- know you have everything you need inside of you
- Be Big and grow tall
- do what you came to do and be, here on Earth

- everyone is Special, Unique, and Very Needed Here on Earth
- We are all Interconnected, I am you and you are me
- As the Mayans said "In Lak'ech Ala K'in".

Instead of playing the Victim role being little and being asked with such attention and sympathy from all the rescuers, people pleasers, and enablers, "Oh, what is wrong? Are you feeling down? I'm sorry, what can I do to help?". Why not be the Creator following your intuition, inner truth and heart and hear, "My you look great and so alive! What are you doing?"

The rescuers mentioned above are only avoiding their own lives by being in someone else's. This keeps them busy. I was a rescuer and very good at it. I'm sure a lot of you are too. The rescuers need to learn to become coaches. They need to quit enabling others to stay in their victim role.

So those two previous paragraphs created some emotion I know. Were you able to identify your emotion, write down your thoughts racing through your brain defying you to catch them, and then maybe excavate the underlying beliefs causing that total ordeal. It is all about changing the brain ruts, which in turn will change your whole reaction to the given scene.

Let's look at this from another angle. What is a disappointment? Would you agree that it is something that did not go as planned? (Are you really free of expectations??) You could say that circumstances, a happening, an action occurred that were out of your control and you are disappointed. (Are you free of trying to control others??) Do you really want to feel disappointed? Why? Could you be judgment free of the situation? Could you control your reaction?? Would you be able to examine the belief causing the thoughts that caused your emotion and reaction? (Are you really resistance free?)

You may be a little confused right now, but read on, please. So let us be the Creator of our life. My lover went out with someone else. Who is responsible for that action? The lover is totally responsible for their actions, not you. Just like a woman is totally responsible for her own orgasms. It is playing a victim role to blame it on your partner.

Do you want to feel betrayed, unloved, unwanted, and wronged as a victim? Do you want to wallow in sadness and pain? Do you want to receive attention and sympathy from your family and friends? Or would it be possible to say Wow, I am so surprised and hurt by your actions. What caused you to do that? What were you thinking? I am going to have to rethink our relationship.

Some beliefs under this for the Victim are marriage until death do us part, monogamy, you betrayed me and I can never trust you again, fault finding, making yourself right, and revenge. Some beliefs under this for the Creator are we are meant to travel together for as long as it works for our mutual healing and growth together, I love myself enough to survive this hurt, my partner is a gift and is an addition to my happiness, and my partner is not responsible for my happiness.

Here is another example. You always have the choice of making drama or being free of drama in your life. Your partner spills red wine on your new light colored carpet. Do you scream? Oh no! You have ruined my new carpet! You idiot! You always bring the incident up years later to blame and try to make your partner feel guilty. Or do you grab the towels and say here let me help you clean that up. You know that accidents happen and your partner feels awful about it. You can drop the incident and release it never to use it against your partner ever again. Do you release and let go of the past? Are you a drama queen? Do you play the victim role of what someone else did?

Victims do not feel they have many choices or much power. A person that was going through money problems and wasn't sure if they could pay their rent might decide they had to live in their car. They might also decide they had to get their windows tinted to prepare for that. There is no other choice in their mind. I would suggest they ask themselves how do I feel. What are my feelings? What thoughts and judgments are coming up? What are the old underlying well rutted beliefs and behavior patterns playing out here?

Here would be some typical responses to the above questions. Please note these are all victim statements. I'm no good and I don't deserve any better. Here I am again failing. Something is wrong with me. I'm worthless. I don't deserve what I want and I'm no good. I'm a failure and I can't do any better. I'm not talented, smart, or intelligent enough. I need help. I don't have help and no one can help me.

The above statements are all excuses. The statements mean I'm not responsible for what happens. Statements of thought are creating the life I'm living right now. Do I want this life? If not, then change your beliefs so you will form different thoughts! That is your mission. Record the opposite non-victim statements in your own voice over and over and play them nightly. Changing a brain rut is like developing one of your body muscles. It takes stimulus, challenge, repetition and practice.

Stand in your personal power. You are in your power when you know in your heart it is right, and you stand alone even when no one agrees with you. You are free of needing someone's approval, when you are in your power. You are free of "needing" a partner. Having personal power, is keeping your power by not giving it to someone else. It is being able to walk alone. It is being able to let go of the past and all the people that no longer support you. Being able to let go of old patterns of behavior and choosing something different, is standing in your power. Standing in your power is being able to see things differently and make change. It is being able to love and take care of your body, emotions, spirit, and mind. Just choose to stand in your power!

CHAPTER 3 - EMOTIONS with Mr. Renaissance

I'm forever indebted to Mr. Renaissance. He possessed such a tenderness and soft deep genuine love. He was very intuitive and understanding of me. We lost ourselves in our lovemaking. It was beyond description. We lost time and presence. As soon as we would see each other we wanted to fall into each other's arms and be consumed. It was mutual and such a fire when Leo and Aires meet. I could "feel" the love from his heart flow to me.

He was very tall and had a big build. He had a very strong personality. I felt protected and safe when I was with him. I knew I was important to him. He was very educated, could speak several languages, knew the arts, loved music, and would tackle and learn anything new he wanted to know or do. Among many other things he was a great cook and proclaimed that food was the language of love. He put love into all of his food preparation.

I'll never forget waking at 2am for intricate delicate flavor melting snacks he'd quickly prepare with drinks of bourbon. It was always heaven again afterwards. He and I will always hold a very special unique close connection formed from many lifetimes together.

I explained to Mr. Renaissance that I came from the remote country lifestyle and had been secluded like that for about seven years, even though living in the big city. He agreed to help educate me back into society, etiquette, and the city life. He took time with detail and always covered my questions. He would make me sit and watch him cook as he delved into another deep teaching topic with me. Then he would serve the food and we would eat in great conversation. He was fantastic and I learned so much from him.

I learned to control my anger that came up when he would correct my grammar or correct me on something else. I realized that came from when I was younger, and felt I never did anything right, and was always scolded or yelled at. I knew he was doing what I had asked him to do and yet I was angry. That didn't make sense until I realized his correcting me was helping me heal some very old wounds I had suppressed at a younger age. I reached the point when he would correct me, that I would say thank you, and laugh that he had caught yet another mistake of mine.

He made me become aware of emotion as it rose in my body. He could instantly make me mad and put me on the defensive. I had to work hard to catch this as it happened. It's like people who fall in the "hole", repeating a routine that they follow everyday with no thought. They are robots following the same way to work, eating the same exact food and not even tasting and feeling it go into their body. They do the exact same job and work every day. They are rote with no feeling. They are ignoring their feelings. They are shrouded, covered, hidden, and masked. They are wearing the mask that they think is expected of them. They are not aware of their choices or emotions anymore.

A very life-saving, helpful, wonderful soul of a fellow coach told me to ask myself when making a decision or choice about something "does this feed me or does this not feed me?" or "does this feel good or this doesn't feel good?". It was such beautiful advice to implement every day.

Most everyone knows that feeling, which is emotion rising in our body when our eyes start to water, and tears are forming, and we want to cry. We start moving our lips, still trying to stop the formation of tears, and holding back the emotion that is flooding our body. Our heart feels sadness or pain, we fall forward to collapse and protect our heart, and we breathe deep trying to stop the tears and the emotion that is rising inside of us. We may have to go have a cigarette. Repeated enough this becomes a rut and easier to do, although it is not in our best healthy interest.

Also known is that feeling when the heat starts rising in our body, our heart beat gets faster and faster, our body tenses, our mind is racing with thoughts, we go on defense and alert, and we start shaking. We know anger has taken over. Just like holding back tears, repeated enough times this also becomes a rut and overtakes us, without us even thinking about it. Our brain has the control over us and our body, instead of us having control of our brain. Our body is on autopilot and our brain is in runaway mode. This is an old repeating behavior and pattern.

I ask you to pay attention to your emotions when they are triggered, and your buttons get pushed and set into motion. Try to stop, look at the situation, breathe slow and deep and listen to your thoughts. Our emotions are the keys to alert us that we have a belief that needs examined and possibly changed. It may be unconscious but it is still your responsibility now to uncover it, and excavate it, and remodel it. Remember it is not the person or event that is the problem here, it is you. I always used the phrase I created in my hardest healing times of: "Feel it, Heal it, Release it". Now we also have: "Feel it, Catch it, Excavate it."

We can always recognize when we are having an emotion by the feeling in our body. Many of us have ignored our body so long, that we are not conscious of how our body really feels. We need to take moments during the day to check in on how our right foot feels. Is it comfortable and if it isn't, what can I lovingly do for myself to make it feel better. Ask yourself, do my hips feel good, are there any pains in my body right now, are my muscles tensed or relaxed, are my shoulders relaxed or drawn toward my ears, and is my chin pointing upward or more downward. You will become more aware of your body and begin to love and care for your body. These questions will most of all help you realize when an emotion is rising and something is happening in your energy field. Please, I ask you to bring your attention inward to your own body during the day and notice what is happening inside yourself. If you are tense, everyone around you will also probably be tense. Emotions and energy feelings are contagious.

All six lanes of traffic are at a dead stop and you are still miles from the airport. Immediately you think I'm going to miss my flight. I can't miss my flight. The emotion of fear takes over your body. Thoughts created by your beliefs are racing unconscious through your brain provoking all kinds of emotions and reactions. Your breathing gets quicker and shallow and your heart rate increases. You are sinking into lower and lower vibrational frequencies. Your body is tensing and you get angry, snappy, and anxious and start having more doom and gloom thoughts. You are no longer in the present moment. You are living in the past (old past conditioning and memories of prior events like this) and living in the future (predicting every disaster that will occur if you miss your flight).

What's the worst that can happen when fear overtakes you? Look for the golden egg in the moment. Fear of missing your flight keeps you from seeing the golden egg that's right before you. See what is right in the moment instead of snapping at the airport shuttle driver what to do and where to turn. You are taking your anger out on him. In other words you are projecting your anger onto him. You are directing your anger at him. Remember energy follows thought.

How would you react if your energy system was open to receiving all the low frequency vibrational energy being directed at you by all the upset people on the shuttle? It could quickly and easily upset you, and at the minimum stress you. However if everyone was supporting you and sending that energy to you, it would be easier for you to solve the problem quicker and more creatively with your experience and expertise.

So would you be able to operate more efficiently with four passengers sending low negative energy vibrations at you or if they were sending supportive, positive and trusting high energy vibrations to you knowing you knew what to do. Remember that we are all connected energetically. A group is stronger than one. There is strength and power in numbers.

So fear causes the body to go into alert and on guard status. You lose control or never had it anyway of your brain, and that control is now taken over by fear and it determines what you are going to do. Fear is now in control of your computer brain. You have given up complete control of yourself to fear. That takes you out of the present moment and pulls you to future and past thoughts. Maybe what is right in this moment is a better question for you than what can happen.

Maybe a change would be to trust and try to find the golden egg before you in the now, instead of reliving past events and playing out future catastrophes. We are trained to jump to the negative and think the worst that can happen. I ask why not retrain ourselves to jump to the best that can happen. Maybe you will meet someone because of the delay that could be a new business partner, a new client, a new employer, or life partner.

There are as many exciting wonderful things that could happen as there are catastrophes. The trick is that if you are not living the present moment they can be touching you on the cheek, literally standing in front of you, speaking to you, and shaking your hand; but you will not even see them because you do not believe they could exist. You will ignore them because your runaway brain is completely filled with living the past and future, and has no room for the present moment to even exist in it.

I imagine you just had all kinds of reasons come up for why that could never be the best way for us to think. A piece inside us rebels strongly and very loudly, when we try to change a deep rut. The same way it is known, that the body craves and wants whatever it is allergic to.

DISSOLVE FEAR

The emotion of fear usually is a liar. True enough at times when we are clear, fear is an asset and alerts us to real danger. However, most of the time fear controls our lives and keeps us from being our authentic self. It keeps us from having fun and enjoying the pleasures of life here on Earth. Declare to yourself that you choose not to believe lies anymore.

Make a list of all of your fears. Now rate them from zero to ten with ten being your greatest and most crippling fear. I suggest that you write these fears in order on sheets of paper starting with 0. A zero fear would be one that sometimes you do, but generally you choose not to. A ten rated fear would be one that you absolutely refuse to attempt to do. It totally has you locked down from enjoying life.

I would like for you to take the first zero fear you listed and do this work with it until it is no longer a fear for you. When it presents itself, notice and write down what your emotions, thoughts, and beliefs had to be for the event to occur. What type of emotion did you feel, and where did you feel it in your body? What thoughts were running in your brain? Then later write down what beliefs would support those thoughts. It is the thoughts that cause your fear, and you believe them. So I suggest you figure out if you still want to have the beliefs that cause those thoughts that control your happiness.

Why not work on the fear of standing naked in front of your partner in the daylight? Wouldn't it feel really great to feel sexy, strong and attractive standing there instead of feeling shame, not good enough, and ugly? I still get amazed at the number of men and women out there that have this fear. Wouldn't it be more fun to play and not be worried about what your partner is thinking about your body? The truth is that the partner is thinking none of what you think they are thinking. It is only your own thoughts keeping you from enjoying the moment. Now will you practice standing in front of the mirror naked, seeing and feeling how beautiful you are? Ok, start with dimmed light if necessary.

Praise yourself on each step. Praise yourself for wanting to change and walk through your fears. Praise yourself for noticing the fear when it comes up. Praise yourself when you finally notice a thought connected to the fear. This process can take some time. Be patient with yourself. Praise and congratulate yourself on each and every step. Let go completely of criticizing yourself. Criticizing ourselves keeps us in fear and feeling unworthy.

Let's undo the old programming and walk through our fears!

DISSOLVE ANGER

The emotion of anger we feel toward someone in the present moment is usually also a lie. True enough at times when we are clear, anger is an asset and alerts us to the real moment at hand. However, most of the time, anger stored from the past controls our lives and keeps us from being our authentic self. It keeps us from having fun and enjoying the pleasures of life here on Earth. Declare to yourself that you choose not to let old stored anger control your life anymore!

Make a list of all of the times you get angry, for example when someone blows their horn at you. Now rate them from zero to ten, with ten being your greatest and most outraging anger. I suggest that you write these angers in order on sheets of paper starting with 0. A zero anger would be one that sometimes you have, but generally you choose not to. A ten rated anger would be one that you absolutely lose control and dip to an all out low vibrational outburst. It totally takes control of you and keeps you from enjoying life in your true authentic calm manner.

I would like for you to take the first zero anger situation you listed and do this work with it until it is no longer an anger causer for you. When it presents itself, notice and write down what your emotions, thoughts, and beliefs were for the event to occur. What type of emotion did you feel and where in your body did you feel it? What thoughts were running in your brain? Then later write down what beliefs would support those thoughts. It is the thoughts that cause your anger and you believe them, but they are generally programmed from the past. You needed them in the past to survive but they are no longer necessary for your survival. We are runaway anger throwing people in the present moment being ruled and controlled from old past mind conditioning. So I suggest you figure out if you still want to have the beliefs that cause those thoughts that control your happiness.

Please understand as you do this exercise that underneath anger is always a hurt, pain, and sadness. Honor that emotion when it comes up. Feel it, Heal it, and Release it! It is from the past, but it needs dealt with so it leaves your energy field and is no longer a block to your energy flow. Once you understand where it originated, you are free of its control over your present moment actions and life. It really is that simple.

Praise yourself on each step. Praise yourself for wanting to change and walk through your angers. Praise yourself for noticing the anger when it comes up. Praise yourself when you finally notice a thought connected to the anger. This process can take some time. Be patient with yourself. Praise and congratulate yourself on each and every step. Let go completely of criticizing yourself. Criticizing ourselves keeps us in anger and feeling unworthy.

Let's undo the old programming and get real with our anger!

Example of this exercise:

I get mad when someone blows their horn at me.

MY EMOTIONS: I feel the anger rise from my gut to my head. I feel my heart beating faster, my breathing quicken and my body tense. I feel ready to fight.

MY THOUGHTS: I think they are judging me. I think they think they are better than me. I think they believe they have control over me and can tell me what to do and when I am wrong. No one has the right to tell me what to do or how to behave. I feel unworthy. I feel lower than them. I was right and they were wrong, and I'll defend myself.

MY BELIEFS: Possibly and most likely formed from a trauma in your life at an earlier age, your unconscious beliefs may include: I am not worthy. I have no control over what happens to me. They have no right to do that to me. This is wrong. I feel trapped and unable to protect myself. I want to protect and defend myself but I can't. In order to survive the trauma we had to stuff our anger because we were too small to protect our self. Or for whatever circumstances, we felt we were unable to protect our self.

Let's look at anger in a different light. It is an emotion and we feel it. Why do we judge anger as wrong and that we shouldn't have or feel it? It's our body talking to us. We don't judge being happy as wrong, so why say I can't feel angry, that's wrong? Now all destructive anger that we send out destroying and aimed at everything within a fifty mile radius of us, being destructive to everything in its path, is not what I am talking about.

I am talking about feeling the anger of the past event that caused that emotion to be felt by us. That is how our body is communicating to us on how to heal our self. We have to feel it, heal it, and then release it. Always underneath anger is being hurt, betrayed or harmed by another. It was real and we need to feel it and not stuff it down in our body. That is how we end up with an illness, if we are always stuffing and denying what we are feeling.

Most of the time as a child, we are taught not to feel our emotions that are judged as wrong by others. Anger is one of those emotions that is judged as wrong to feel, as is sadness sometimes. I suggest you let that anger come out in a constructive way so your body can heal. Have a private conversation by yourself pretending that the event or person that caused that emotion is in front of you. They cannot talk, but you can say everything you need to say to them. Dig into it. Understand and feel it. Release it and let it go. Fill the event and yourself with love and lots of love. This is a necessity if you want to heal.

Write out your anger unrestricted. Then tear it up and burn it. Find constructive ways of releasing your stored anger. Chop wood or beat and scream into a pillow until the anger moves from your system and you feel the tears of release from the hurt flow from your body. This actually does help the blockage in the energy field release itself. Buy a cheap set of dishes and go throw them against a wall in the garbage pit. Don't let it eat away at your precious being until you develop an illness like I did. Speak your truth if only in private. It still works and is ridding your body of the infestation you've been stuffing and letting manifest into the angry destructive force within you. This is very healing and so freeing.

Thoughts are energy. Every time you have a thought energy follows it. Energy follows thought. What you give out is what you create. Emotions are energy in motion. You can let emotions flow through your body or you can hold onto them or create blockages in your energy flow. Layer upon layer of negative emotions that are not allowed to move through the body, will eventually create a problem in the physical body, and can result in serious diseases or illnesses. They eventually become toxins at the cellular level. Lower vibrational frequency energy has to be transmuted by higher frequency energy. Therefore, the Quippet!

Emotions and states of being that have light very high fast vibrational frequencies are love, joy, peace, serenity, wellness, good health, positive thoughts, positive emotions, positive beliefs, positive action, enthusiasm, cheerfulness, faith, kindness, blissfulness, confidence, worthiness, harmony, calm, abundance, wonder, inspiration and courage. These are contagious. When you get one you start collecting the others.

Hate, illness, disease, war, worry, anxiousness, panic, fear, victim, failure, pity, blame, doubt, unkindness, depression, insecurity, worthlessness, negative thoughts, negative emotions, negative beliefs, loneliness, rage, impoverishment, cowardice, and boredom have very dense low slow vibrational frequencies. The same is true here. These are contagious. When you get one you start collecting the others. Do you want to collect high frequency vibrations or low frequency vibrations? Be selective, be present, and be aware in your actions. Do not let your run away brain control your life. Use your brain as the computer in service to you as it was meant to be.

There are many charts out there depicting the low and high vibrational frequency emotions, but I think you get the idea with the ones I listed. Some people believe only two basic emotions exist, and all others branch off of these, and those are love and fear. Others believe there are four basic emotions being happy, fear, anger, and sadness. I just want you to become aware of the emotion when it occurs in your body. Take notice and say to yourself I am having an emotion.

I want you to control your brain and leave everyone else alone. The people in your life are only a reflection of how you are treating yourself. That's what people mean when they say your life is a reflection of yourself. If you are always around angry situations, then why not quit being angry and upset with yourself.

If you have a lot of people lying to you, look inside yourself and find the many ways you are probably lying to yourself. Do you say I am going to start being on time only to not be on time again. Do you tell yourself you will get more sleep, but you don't? That is lying to yourself and breaking your word to yourself. Therefore, you will attract people into your life that "reflects" that to you, to bring it to your attention to work on.

Let's look at the emotions raised when someone is late for an appointment. We feel frustration that we are not starting on time, that we have to wait on someone to make their appearance, and we feel discounted because we arrived on time, yet we have to wait on the others.

May I also add here that showing up late only shows other people that we totally disrespect them and their time, that we have a need for getting attention, that we feel more important than them, that we feel we are busier than they are and that we have some issues that we need to look at. I have great compassion for these people because their actions are generally very unconscious, deeply rutted patterns of behavior. If you are one of these people, please be very patient and loving with yourself as you look at this behavior. You may need to seek some support in unraveling what is causing you to behave in this way

We see other people through "our filters" and until those filters are cleared; we don't see that person for who they are at all. Therefore, we need to tend to our own business and no one else's. As they say there is only my business, your business, and the Universe's business.

Don't try to help and control others. Until you get some clarity, helping others can be a way of distracting yourself from your own issues and life. Our business is only controlling our own brain and our own thoughts.

Don't let your brain control you anymore unless you want to stay where you are in life. You want to change your life? Then let me repeat, get control of your brain and the thoughts it produces! It is that simple.

In my opinion our lives in this world are controlled by runaway brains. We are robots so unaware of our actions most of the time. The runaway brains controlling us are filled with everyone else's beliefs and not always ours. We need to be aware of what our thoughts are and control them, so they are positive and based on beliefs we really believe in.

For an exercise, if you want one, write down how many places you have wanted to visit but haven't and the reasons why you haven't gone there. Do you always stay in a thirty to fifty mile radius of where you live? Do you have a set pattern of places you go? Do you drive the same route to a place each and every time you go there? How many of you want a different career, a different car, a different mate? Write down your wants and why you haven't gone after them. Are there really any reasons besides fear and lack?

One belief I still have trouble changing is that there is plenty of time. I catch myself saying I don't have enough time and exhibiting stress and anxiety. I have too much to do. There is never enough time. It has been a very deep rut in my brain that I'm still trying to fill up and replace with a new rut. There is an abundance of time, help and resources if only we believe there is. Many people understand that time doesn't even exist, it is just a concept used on Earth to facilitate life here.

Repeat the affirmation I am worthy of receiving all good things I desire. Without desire, we have no life. Think of the retired people you know that their life energy is gone. They have no life. A person must have passion and desire to live fully. Life's spectrum runs from a dead robot life to a full driving life that is full of desire. Which one are you living?

I ask you to pay attention to your emotions when they are triggered or set into motion. Our emotions are the keys to alert us that we have a belief that needs examined and changed. It may be unconscious, but it is still your responsibility now to uncover and excavate it and remodel it. Remember it is not the person or event that is the problem here, it is you. I am repeating again that I always used the phrase I created in my hardest healing times of: "Feel it, Heal it, Release it". Now we also have: "Feel it, Catch it, Excavate it."

If you are in denial and not noticing your emotions, your life is stuck and not changing. You have the same fights, disappointments and arguments over and over. You are probably stuffing and ignoring your emotions with certain activities like binge eating, just over eating, over working, always on your phone, addicted to social media, other addictions like shopping, drugs, gambling, drinking, staying busy at all times, never sitting still, anything you do excessively to distract yourself from feeling your emotions. These same fights, disappointments and arguments follow you to new relationships and new places to live. The problem is inside you and how you are treating yourself, not where you live or who you are with.

I smoked cigarettes for many years. I used cigarettes when I was stressed, angry, wanting to relax, overworked, emotional, feeling uneasy, not wanting to cry, and especially when I was trying to stuff any emotion away and get rid of it. I was smoking three packs a day for several months before I was able to try and quit.

At these times when you feel a need to suppress a feeling or don't want to feel it, try asking yourself the following questions in order and honestly answer them.

1. What emotion am I feeling? How does it make me feel? What am I thinking about it?
2. What thoughts would cause that emotion or emotional response?
3. What beliefs would cause those thoughts? Are those beliefs still true for me?
4. Do I want to change that belief? If so, how?
5. Always know that when you are changing something you will be tested until you get it down pat.

If you stay in denial of your feelings and emotions long enough, they may well manifest into physical symptoms in your body like mine did. It will start as a slight pain, annoying catch, little headache, sleep problems or many other possible ways. The symptoms will grow and increase as you deny and stuff your emotions.

They are first blockages in the energetic fields of the body and then later manifest into the physical body. We are energy before we are physical matter as I have stated before. As the symptoms manifest in the physical body they can turn into a full blown illness.

We as a society reward illness and suffering, and all but encourage it. We give pills to cover the physical symptoms instead of trying to find and correct the cause. At times these pills literally cause more breakdowns, and facilitate other illnesses in the physical body. At other times, these same pills save lives.

When our brains register that it is acceptable for a possible side effect of a drug to be death, are we still thinking for ourselves? Have we allowed software programming of our own brain to be done by someone else? Yes, others can and have programmed your brain and may continue to do so, if you don't take control of your own brain and life. Please understand that I am not stating that prescription drugs and modern medicine is not necessary for our health because it is when used appropriately. It is totally life saving at times. I am just asking you to be sure that your decision is feeding you or know that it is not feeding you, and to be aware of any beliefs controlling this decision.

CHAPTER 4 - HUMAN BODY with Mr. Geronimo

Mr. Geronimo, a Virgo, was a better lover than your imagination could ever dream of. He was such a unique and very wise old soul at a very early age in Earth life. He was the epitome of physical fitness without the use of steroid drugs or other artificial help. He was all natural. He was tall and had a very muscular sexy body. Oh yes! He was the strongest fittest man I'd ever been with. He could pick me up and place me against the wall while making wild tender love to me. Any female's dream! I was in ecstasy. Not only was he strong physically, he was strong emotionally, mentally and spiritually. He knew who he was and lived by his own code of ethics, which I admired so much.

Our first meeting was record breaking. He took me out for a drink and then we went grocery shopping where he picked everything including the red wine with such care. Please note that I love men that cook well and make love well. We arrived back at my place and went swimming for awhile. We returned to my room and then showered together. Need I say what that lead to? The shower towel bar broke at one point and it was tossed to the side. I have never had love made to me like that in a shower before or even since then. He set the bar very high. He was an excellent lover. He was aggressive, strong and passionate like we Aries love and need at times.

Mr. Geronimo was an excellent cook. He was all into what was good for our bodies. He cooked the best steak and kale I've ever eaten or ever will eat because we were in that "special space and time of being so present with each other and enjoying the moment". Those "moments" occur when you are fully grounded/present in your human body, and experiencing what I call an elevated dimension of human life.

He cooked with intentional presence and filled the food with love. Food really is the language of love. The food melted in our mouths with warmth and love flooding our bodies. That day was monumental. The red wine was so delicious. We continued to make more passionate vigorous love on through the night. We smoked an American Spirit. My first cigarette I had smoked since 1994. This was a cigarette of total enjoyment, sweetness, and satisfaction. Anyone that has ever smoked, knows what I am talking about.

This fantasy surpasses anyone's imagination and deserves recognition. I have to also state that I was so thankful and grateful to my personal trainer at this point. I had the physical strength and stamina in my body that allowed me to stay up with such a fit younger man. The most memorable and best lovemaking I've ever had except of course for the subsequent sessions with him.

This young man was so deep and advanced in his thoughts and actions. He saw things so clearly and could state them in very few words directly making the point clear. He had an imagination that surpassed many. He was so creative. He was worldly and nothing you said really shocked him. It was like he already knew it and was glad you had finally reached the point of seeing it.

He was "remembering" in a faster manner than I had ever witnessed with anyone before. All that had to be done was for the subject to be mentioned and a few minutes discussion about it and he "remembered" it all. It was like he instantly downloaded generations of info by just saying a keyword and integrated it all within a few days. He would be talking on the subject like a pro, when he had only heard about it a few days before.

This man has so many special gifts that he was utilizing without even really being fully aware of it. But that is what makes him so humble and real. His heart is huge and he can read people like a book. These are the kind of people who have come to Earth to make a difference. He is doing his work, learning his gifts and how to best utilize them to help people.

Mr. Geronimo loves learning all about the human body all the way from the mitochondria to the ways we interact socially. He experiments with his own body learning how muscle develops. He knows that each and every one of us is a very unique being. This leads me into the chapter about our magnificent human body and how it interacts with our spiritual being.

We are energy beings first. I believe we are eternal as energy beings or in spirit form as some people refer to it. Then we inhabit (are born into) the physical body to be able to function and be on Earth. Many believe we should cry when we are born and celebrate when we transition. Our physical bodies are miracles beyond our imagination. I don't believe we fully yet understand how magnificent they are. I hope by the end of my book you will be treating your body as one of your miracles that you have been graciously given.

Yes, I believe we sign a contract which includes who our parents will be, what we came to do, what our gifts will be, what our name will be, and all the points of our life even when we will transition. This is all mixed in with free choice which allows for different pathways through our life. Of course, at birth we forget ALL of this. There is no rush. We never get it all done. If we did……what then? Lighten up and enjoy the physical body. Here on Earth we get to feel, see, smell, hear, and taste. Oh, what luxuries the senses of the human body are! Stay in the present moment and enjoy life!

We are energetic beings. We are energy. Everything is energy. Everyone knows everything on some level. There are no secrets. Freedom and peacefulness come with opening your secret closet. When you can be an open book in front of anyone, not hiding anything, then you can really relax. To relax is to be what they call grounded. We all perform much more effectively and with much less effort when we are centered and grounded and flowing in the river of life. We all read each other energetically all the time.

People say, and it is true that energy follows thought. For some to understand this, I have rephrased it to say "your body and life follows your thought" or simply "body and life follows thought". Why not believe:

- I look fabulous naked,
- I am rich,
- I am handsome,
- I am beautiful,
- I am creative,
- I am intelligent,
- I am healthy,
- I am successful,
- I am happy,
- I am sexy,
- I am soft and sweet,

- I am love,
- I am loved,
- I am a specimen of perfect health,
- I am a good role model for others,
- I love my life.

We signed up for this. We are Warriors changing the life on Earth.

It is an exciting time now and it is moving fast.

We are role models for others…..each and every one of you that have read this book.

It is time to heal and get on with your job here.

We are role models always…..as we heal, as we crash, as we cry, as we laugh …..Always affecting others…..

Take responsibility for your Life.

Stand up and be seen for who you are and for what you came to do this lifetime!

Our body is pure energy as are all solid objects. We emanate layers of energy that are sometimes labeled as physical, emotional, mental, spiritual, and the layers continue outward. The layers interact and flow with each other. (EVERYTHING is energy and therefore has a vibrational frequency whether it is higher or lower.) We witness illness and aging in the human body.

So what is illness? It is our body's way of letting us know that something is wrong or rather you have not been paying attention to yourself. You have been ignoring precious warning signs your body has been giving you. When the body has no other avenue of getting your attention to help it, it may form an illness which if left unattended, will most likely lay you on your back. Once the body has you on your back, unable to do anything else, you have to deal with the body. It will say, now I have your attention and you must help me out here. We are going to transform this situation.

In my opinion, illness is total disregard of your human body. You have ignored all the warning signs your body has been sending to you. Actually, as a society, we are taught that is the righteous strong way of living. You are looked upon as a real hard courageous worker, if you work through a headache or pain in your body day after day and don't miss work. Illness occurs when the body is being ignored by you, and it is in a deteriorating situation.

A deteriorating situation in the body starts when energy blockages are not dealt with and start growing in number. The body will function at a high level even with some blockages, although not at the premium level. However, when the energy flow really starts being disrupted, the symptoms grow in number and intensity. That small ache becomes a slight limp, followed by a real noticeable limp. You may even need a cane to help you walk. In reality this is an energy blockage that you are not healing and releasing. The light shortness of breath, slight dizziness and twinge of a chest pain left unattended, can put you in the hospital with a full blown heart attack.

These physical changes usually appear slowly over time, and you tend to adapt and live with them, as your new level of accepting less than optimum health. We have labeled it aging. Think of all the beliefs out there that we are getting old and it is accepted to start having physical pains and feeling less than optimum health every day. I believe we can transition feeling, moving, playing, thinking, and looking much more youthful or better than we think we can. Do you see where our meaning of age appropriate may need to be re-evaluated?

When we allow our body to reach this level of illness then we must attend to the physical body first and foremost. However, treating the symptoms and not the cause, is not a permanent healing of the illness. You may get the blood pumping again through your heart by several different surgical methods, but unless you heal the underlying emotional, mental, and spiritual causes of your heart malfunction, you will not be healed. You will be temporarily fixed. You have only put a band aid on the spot when there is really a deep infection growing. The body's heart will flare up again trying to get healed. It may take a few weeks or even a few years, but it will more than likely come back eventually.

Now I must also mention at this point, once again, the magnificence of the human body. If by some means when you had the heart attack you were also able to heal the energetic blockage in your energy field that was creating this condition, then you could be permanently healed of this condition. In other words, "Feel it, Heal it, and Release it". So, if this occurred your body would be totally capable of healing that infection growing under the band aid, most likely without even letting you know it was there. The physical body is capable of healing instantly, if all the root causes are healed.

I would like to state this again a little differently. Illness starts in the energetic field and for complete healing the energetic field must be restored by physical, emotional, mental and spiritual healing. The energy body exists before the physical body and everything in the energetic body eventually filters down into the physical body when allowed to build up as a blockage of energy flow. When allowed to filter into the physical body that is when the physical symptoms start and will continue to grow in intensity if not attended to. The energy field is where it all starts and ends.

The physical body restores and heals itself. It knows how to heal itself, if we support and let it. The body is truly a miracle housing for our spirit. However, unless we heal all the fields (i.e. physical, emotional, mental, and spiritual) we will not be cured and the illness may easily stay and control our life, or we "use the illness to control" others and become a professional illness person, or we allow it to disintegrate our very existence without healing. If we choose to do the hard work of healing our energetic fields, the rewards are unspeakable. The work in a nutshell is listening to our emotions, discovering their underlying thoughts, then discovering and changing the underlying beliefs causing those emotions. Walk through your fear. "Feel it, Catch it, Excavate it." It is life changing.

I want to add here that the past ways of healing the emotions is evolving into much quicker, easier methods as we move forward in time on Earth. Each and every trauma does not have to be excavated and relived. We are creators not victims. Our intention to heal and release blockages plays a huge role in how smoothly this can be accomplished as well as our "beliefs" of how this transpires. Clear yourself let your energy flow and be the Warrior you came here to be.

Beliefs cause Thoughts that cause Emotion.

Change your Beliefs and that changes your thoughts which in turn changes your Emotions.

Release the Energy Blockages and let your Energy Flow.

So what is aging? Every 7-10 years our body is totally renewed. DNA can be changed! DNA is not stagnant once we are born with it! The best ageless remedies I can give you are to heal your beliefs, let your emotions flow, and release the energy blockages in your system. By doing this it allows the new cell being reproduced by the body to be rejuvenated and more nearly perfect every seven years instead of replicating the old saddened damaged cell that is still not free to change.

Ageless is not the newest beauty cream or treatment out on the market but rather a release of old trapped energy in your energetic body. Heal your old buried wounds. You will feel and look much younger. Feel it. Heal it. Release it.

When an event happens we need to feel, express, and release the emotion that rises so that a blockage isn't created in our energy system. For example if your house burns down, you need to feel all the emotions and mentally, physically, spiritually, and emotionally release them. Everyone is unique and different but this might mean taking fifteen minutes and crying, screaming, expressing verbally, safely expressing physically all the emotions being felt so that they are released fully and nothing gets stored in your energy field. I challenge you not to be the victim of the situation.

Extreme attempts at trying to stay young are being in denial or fear of transitioning. I prefer to use the word transitioning instead of death because of all the connotations we as a society have with the words death and dying. The fact is that we travel for a while on Earth in a human body then we leave. Lots of people believe we return many lifetimes as in reincarnation. My software states that we do not have to accept the beliefs that our Earth body has to deteriorate as we get older. My software has been programmed to believe we can feel young and be actively young until we transition.

Remember that fear is an emotion created only by our thoughts which come from our beliefs. I believe this poem states what I am talking about so clearly.

> There is fear on top of the mountain,
>
> There is fear in the deep Black Sea,
>
> There is fear that is inescapable,
>
> Because it all comes from inside of me.
>
> ......Roy MacDonald

I have faced death. I woke one morning and had to be taken to the emergency room. Within less than two hours after waking they had me in the emergency room and had called the Chaplin in to give last rites. I was looking down from the ceiling at myself on the ER bed. I did see the light that everyone talks about, and it was extraordinary and beyond description. Within the exact same seconds, I heard my daughter calling me back and saying I could not leave her on Earth alone right now. Knowing she was right, I returned to my body. My daughter was not at the hospital. It took me about five months of bed rest and another seven months to recover fully where I could walk two miles easily.

A few years later my body had deteriorated to the point that I could not literally add two plus two, walk by myself, bathe myself, go to the bathroom by myself, feed myself, dress myself, I was having four to six seizures a day that were lasting from sixty to ninety minutes each, and I was told face to face by the medical doctor there was nothing more they could do for me. I was facing death. It took me seven long hard years to recover. I speak from firsthand experience about the things I discuss in this book.

Now maybe you understand more fully why I am concerned about people who want to leave Earth, but are not sure if it is really their contractual time to do so. I think I'm done trying to transition before it is my time. I make light of it now and I say, "They won't let you leave until it is your time, because I have tried and I know." Yes, I am a Warrior and I have been put to the tests. Many more tests than I have revealed in this book. But I have survived and am now uncovering my inner jewel and starting to work my dream. I do speak from my own life experience. Everything in my book is the unexaggerated truth of my experience. Only the men in my book are imaginary. I created them as I lay ill in bed. However, they are real to me when I need them.

So maybe your physical body is in good shape and you haven't ever been ill. Do you feel fulfilled emotionally, mentally and spiritually? Or do you feel there has to be more to life? What is life? Why am I here? Will I ever be happy? What's wrong with me? Why can't I feel happy all the time? Why can't I get motivated? How can I do what I really want to do? Others are doing it. Why can't I? Am I being punished? Am I not good enough? What did I do wrong? Am I too lazy? I feel trapped in this relationship, in this life. My partner doesn't get it, or have the same motivation and desire that I have. I have to stay with my partner because of the kids, of money, of insurance, and on and on the excuses continue.

I promise you......LIFE CAN BE DIFFERENT FOR YOU......keep reading.

Red Wine and Cigarettes   *Kathy D. Carter*

CHAPTER 5 - TOOLS with Mr. Backup

Chapter 5 is bringing together the tools that you can use to change your life. That reminds me of an endearing wonderful soul Mr. Backup, a Sagittarius. He was always there when I needed him. He was just the right height and knew how to use what he had. You know what I mean by that. He was gorgeous, alluring, witty, fun, easy, muscular, organized, in control and he could casually accomplish in a day what others took a week to do. He was always present, watching details and still multitasking with ease as he gave me full attention.

Mr. Backup had such a wonderful open, giving, caring heart. He also lived free of judgment most of the time. He listened to every word I uttered whether important or not. He was eager to learn all about me. He soaked in every detail, like he was studying all women kind. I really think he was. He was learning me inside and out.

I'll never forget the time he entered the door and just started kissing me and backed me into the wall. He held my arms above my head with one hand while he touched and explored me with his other hand and kissed me the whole time. He then started leading me to the bedroom when he stopped and picked up the dining table stool and sat it against the wall. He proceeded to sit down and pulled me in front of him. That was one love making session I will not forget. It was other earthly. He always had tender, loving, engaging pillow talk after our love making sessions. He was special!

He was so open, so loving, and went with the moment. He was spontaneous and fully giving and fun, but dominating in a way that was easy and made me feel good yet without the control. If I ever wanted a husband and father, he would most definitely be my first choice. He was fun! He could instantly, calmly and wonderfully solve any problem that arose. He knew how to access and use all the tools available to him in life.

One of the easiest and most fun tools that Mr. Backup always reminded me of was looking at things in a light happy way. He could make me laugh over the most serious deep conversation, issue at hand, or topic. Laughter is one of the best tools we have for releasing energy blockages in our energy fields. There are groups that meet up just to laugh. It is healing. You know how good you feel after laughing so hard that tears roll down your cheeks. Laughter is truly healing. Find and create more ways each day to laugh full heartedly. Go have some fun!

On the same spectrum, tears are also very healing and will release blockages in your energy fields. It is necessary to cry for good health. It is our body's way of releasing toxins and blockages. Now I am not talking about crying in self pity and feeling sorry for yourself. We have no use for pity tears. They come from the victim.

I never wanted to cry because I knew it would never end. A movie could cause me to start crying but I couldn't stop. After many years, I now understand why. I had bottled up my tears for so long that if my body found a chance to release, it took it. Therefore, I would end up bawling way too long when a couple minute silent cry was much more appropriate. I avoided going to watch sad or tear provoking movies in public for that reason. I would not attend funerals. Now days, I can cry for five to ten seconds and release the emotion. I have never been able to cry for less than many long minutes once the tears started, ever before in my entire life. I did not think it was even possible to cry for under thirty minutes, or two hours, or longer. It is liberating to be able to feel emotion and release it as it happens, and not try and stuff away those tears. Stuffing tears is a lot of hard work that is unhealthy.

Please start being AWARE of the thoughts you are having, and what you are saying to yourself. Everything I say in this book is purposeful in many ways. You may judge it, you may dislike it, you may feel offended, you may feel surprised, you may feel relief that someone else thinks the same way as you, or whatever else you may think and feel as you read. Sometimes what I say is to keenly and awkwardly make you aware of your thoughts. Until you start paying attention to what you are thinking, i.e. your thoughts, what I suggest as tools for changing your life will not be helpful to you.

I give you the same and different lists with different wording and presentation to try and help as many people as I can. We are all unique and different. This book and the words in it carry lots of healing energy. Everyone learns in a different manner. Here is a list of a few helpful tools:

- Please start replacing I "can't" with I "won't" in your statements every day.
- Each morning get into character, go to the mirror and look yourself in the eye, then out loud admire and say I love you, stating your name, and feel genuine emotional love for yourself. Feel the emotion flow through your body.
- Find others of like mind and make an agreement to playfully catch each other in negative thoughts and say we need a quippet now. "Quippet me. Take me higher!" Make it fun!
- Daily state out loud something new you are grateful for.
- Kiss and hug yourself daily.

I always learn and understand something better with real live examples, so I will share one here with you. I asked myself what do I really want, and I started writing a list. Here is most of the list.

- Strong self-confidence, self-esteem, strong core
- Deep loving, fun connection with a male partner—my "dream lover"
- Engaging, creative, fulfilling work that is a lot of fun
- A few committed close intimate friends
- Freedom to do it my way
- Freedom of guilt, should have, ought to, need to, doing wrong, FEAR
- Be charismatic, bright diamond sparkling light, alluring and sexy
- Have a friendly upbeat staff supporting and working for and with me that are close, excellent, trustworthy, dependable, accurate and loving their work
- To use this free time wisely to start my dream work while maintaining steady 24 hour cash flow
- If in My Highest Good a working partner preferably my special "dream lover"
- Fun, parties, travel, lots of time doing personal care, beautiful gardens, pool, time sharing with friends
- Hungry audiences for my teachings
- Eager dedicated students

- Art and photo showings with great demand for my items because people are so helped and healed with them
- Feel satisfaction, fulfillment and joy at the end of each day.

So next I looked at the list and asked myself the questions about my relationship with my own Inner Self. Here is that list.

- Do I trust myself and have a strong relationship with my Inner Self?
- Do I have a deep love for myself?
- Am I engaging, creative and satisfied with myself?
- Am I behaving as a close intimate friend to myself?
- Do I give my Inner Self freedom to do it her way?
- Do I allow my Inner Self freedom from criticism, feeling guilt, should haves, ought tos, need tos, and fear?
- Do I allow my true inner essence to be and show it to others?
- Am I close, accurate, dependable and trustworthy when I work with my Inner Self?
- Do I work wisely with my Inner Self and believe everything will be provided?
- Do I trust that things happen in my Highest Good?
- Am I a good working partner with my Inner Self?
- Do I provide parties, travel, pool, personal care, and beauty for my Inner Self?
- Am I a hungry audience for my Inner Self's wisdom?
- Am I an eager dedicated student for my Inner Self?
- Do I show and give great demand and appreciation for my art, photo, intuitive and healing abilities?
- Do I feel proud, satisfied, fulfilled and joyful with myself at the end of the day?

My next step was to write my affirmations and see what emotions/reactions I felt. So here is a list of my affirmations.

- I have a deep love and trust for myself.
- I am an engaging, creative, satisfied person.

- I am treating myself like a close intimate friend would.
- I give my Inner Self freedom to do it her way.
- I praise, support, trust and encourage my Inner Self in what she wants.
- I am accurate, dependable, and trustworthy for my Inner Self in allowing her to be and show her true inner essence.
- I work wisely with my Inner Self and know I have everything I need already inside me.
- I know everything happens for my Highest Good.
- I provide play, parties, travel, water fun, beauty and personal care for my body and Inner Self.
- I am hungry to learn and carry out what my Inner Self wants from me.
- I am a great intuitive of valuable healing information for people.
- I am very happy, satisfied, and ok with whom I am. I am ok.

Now I want to outline this helpful tool for you.

1. Write down what you want.
2. Go through this list and pick out the key words and phrases.
3. Look at your relationship with yourself.
4. What you observe in your relationship with yourself is what is reflected as your life each and every day!!
5. Next write your affirmations from your list. Observe and take notice of what emotions and reactions that you feel as you create your affirmations.

Here is the same tool presented in a different way.

INNER SELF

My Inner Self whispers wisdom to me

(I ignore the loud demanding repeating wants of my Ego.)

ME

Day to Day in Body

How I treat myself

OUTER SELF

The life I'm creating

The life I'm creating outside of me

- Just ask. Ask your Inner Self to help you internalize these new beliefs. Repeat them as often as a good friend would suggest who was dedicated to helping you change. Live them. Feel them to the core of your body. Be considerate, understanding, and gentle with yourself when you catch yourself in the old ruts. Be proud that you caught yourself and just rephrase it. Set your intention daily to live by your new beliefs.

- Remember your ego will not like the change of old ways and will try to sabotage your best efforts. However, after a few tests from the ego where you set the boundary and turn it around, the ego will go to rest. It is like a child who learns that throwing a fit does not always get them what they want. Or you may allow the tantrum throwing two year old to control your destiny. It is your choice and free will.

- All you need to do to change your life is find what is right in this moment! Raise the vibrational frequency. A quippet is any action that makes you feel INSTANTLY better and is on your phone! It must be on your phone because your phone is with you 24/7 and it gives you instantaneous access to your quippet. That is necessary in order for a quippet to do its work.

In my opinion the quickest way to fill in an old brain rut is with quippets. Everyone has time to do a quippet! If nothing else is learned from my book, I hope you learn to breathe correctly and automatically do quippets when you need them. I hope people will start saying, Oh we need a quippet here when the talk has gone negative, or someone is feeling sorry for themselves, playing victim, or someone is gossiping and complaining. Please quippet me now. Take me higher!

Quippets are a way to break the energy of the moment and raise its vibrational frequency to a higher and higher level. A Quippet instantly makes you laugh, smile and feel good! You heal when you stay in higher vibrational frequencies. That is why sitting out in nature feels good and may help you understand your life, situation, or find a solution to your problem more easily. Please quippet me. Take me higher!

The key to a quippet is that you stop instantly upon catching yourself having a negative judgmental thought of low vibrational frequency, and inserting at least one quippet at that moment. This will disrupt the brain rut pattern and help form a new rut of higher vibrational frequency, so that you remain happy and healthy in life.

Examples of Quippets:

- 30 seconds of dancing
- 30 seconds of upbeat music
- 30 seconds of jumping jacks
- 30 seconds of singing
- 30 seconds of laughing
- 30 seconds of deep breathing
- 30 seconds of meditating
- 30 second video that makes you laugh uncontrollably and feel happy
- Petting an animal
- Hugging someone
- Looking in the mirror and saying I love you
- Looking in the mirror and saying you have beautiful eyes, skin, teeth, smile

- Looking in the mirror and saying you are beautiful/handsome and mean it
- Asking and answering "What is RIGHT and GOOD in THIS very moment?
- Stating something you are grateful for
- Looking at an uplifting picture (your children, pets, flowers, scenery, loved ones, etc)
- 30 seconds of whatever makes you "Feel Good"
- Repeating I'm happy, I'm worthy, I'm good, I'm creative
- Use pictures, recordings, mind movies, affirmations, body movement, kissing, hugging

We need to be searching for what makes us feel good. A close friend reminded me, however, that is has to be seen through "objective reality". For example as of now, Scotty can't beam us up, and we can't fly off a building, or climb like spider man because our collective belief system does not support these actions. When we don't feel good, we are out of balance with ourselves. That's why we will lie. We lie in order to try and stay in balance. Telling lies is another book for another time.

Balance in everything is all important. For instance we need to balance work, sleep and rest, play and fun. We need equal amounts of these by the week's end if we can't achieve it daily, which in my opinion is much healthier.

Several people are now learning how to achieve work and play at the same time. That is my intention for this book. I want to help you discover and live your dream. That is what you came to Earth to do. Learn what your own special unique talents and creativity are that you came here with and let them flow. Discover your inner jewel.

If you did not have to think about any responsibilities and having money to pay bills, to eat and to provide shelter, what would you want to be doing right now? Assume you have all the education, money and abilities that you need. What do you do that makes you lose track of time? What have you always dreamed of doing?

Think about what you do that causes you to lose total "control" of time.

You don't even think about time until someone brings it to your attention, or your own inner guidance causes you to look at the clock and say Oh my, look at what time it is. Where did the time go? Look how late it is. Goodness time flies by fast. Oh I have to quit and go do such and such now. These are all statements that will point you toward your inner jewel.

Ladies, you know that precious large carat clear cut diamond you have dreamed of? Men, you know that sports car you have dreamed of? It is just inside of you waiting to be discovered and brought out into the sunlight so it can sparkle. You don't even have to drive to Arkansas to try and find a diamond. It is inside of you. You carry it with you and always have. Your inner jewel is that work which you came here to do. Only you can do it the way you do it. It is your special talent.

Your inner jewel can be anything. It's what makes you light up and feel wonderful. You feel accomplishment and satisfaction. You want to continue doing more of it. You have fun and you get more creative ideas while you are doing it. You don't want to stop and sometimes you don't. Sometimes you work for many hours straight without a break and don't even notice or feel tired afterwards. Sometimes you feel more energized than when you started. Take notice of these wonderful feelings and emotions, because they are helping you discover and uncover your own special inner jewel that no one else can duplicate.

Your own inner jewel has your very own essence in it. You know how you read or hear about others that you admire because it's obvious they love what they're doing, and they sparkle and radiate such a loving warm feeling to everyone. They are living in balance with their inner jewel. They have found and know how to live in balance with life, their inner self, their physical body, their emotional body, their mental body, their spiritual body, and of course their inner jewel. Life only continues to get better and better as you start learning to live in this balance.

Follow the clues you are given if you aren't aware of your inner jewel. If you lose track of time tying knots, reading, gazing at the stars, repairing items, gluing sticks together, or relaxing while feeling a soft breeze on your body just take note and pay attention. Continue to do the activity, and you will be lead to more clues to help you discover your inner jewel.

Something will happen. A word may flash in front of you. You may have a vivid dream. You will get a thought that may seem unrealistic. Just don't discard it. Listen to it. Try it out. Be open minded. Make it a treasure hunt and this is just another clue your Inner Self is giving you. Please don't "discard" anything that comes up or that happens. Be present, alert, and pay close attention. You are on your way to becoming what you've always desired to be deep inside yourself.

The dirtier our filters are, the longer it MAY take us to discover our inner jewel. Others know their jewel, but keep it buried because of their dirty filters and/or because of their fear of taking responsibility for who they could really be.

We must be willing and courageous enough to know we are responsible, and only us, for the way our life unfolds. Take on the responsibility of being the Warrior. Live our dream. Be an example for everyone else. Isn't it our only real duty to perform in this life? Blossom into the flower we were meant to be. Grow into the strong tree and show others how to do it by your example. Show gratitude to those who have done it.

When we are living in balance with our Inner Jewel, healing occurs because the body is in higher vibrational frequencies of joy, love and gratitude. It is hard to stay in a lower frequency when you are being creative in the way that fulfills you and makes you enjoy life to the maximum. Lower vibrational frequencies CANNOT exist in a reality where higher vibrational frequencies are present. Just like darkness cannot exist where there is light.

One very important tool for enjoying life is to feel satisfied and grateful with what you have. Sure you can want and desire more, but just be content and grateful in this moment. You have so much. Are you able to see, breathe without help, touch, feel, love, smell, walk, hug, kiss, shake hands, taste, appreciate, smile, think, hear, dance, move, share, and laugh? Then please find time to feel gratitude for that and relish the moment. Gratitude definitely holds a higher vibrational frequency.

Another tool for reaching a higher vibrational frequency is meditation which can be performed in so many different ways. There is no one right way to meditate. It is like I mentioned earlier in this book. There are a million different flavors of chocolate. Find the one you like and that works for you. Everyone is very unique and different. We do not all have to conform to one way of meditation. The means and results of meditation are different for all of us.

When we get quiet our subconscious tries to let go of things that need healed and set free. That is why so many people claim they do not like to be alone, be still and be quiet, because they do not want to face this necessary healing that the body needs to do to be healthy. They chose to continue to suppress more and more inside, until as some people describe it, the soda bottle explodes.

Meditation can be as simple as counting backwards from one thousand or five thousand. You can later get more focused by counting backwards using your breath. On the in-breath as the belly expands count two and as you let that breath out say hundred. On the next following in-breath count ninety and on the out breath think nine. So it has taken you two inhales and two exhales to say 299. Your next count will be 298 and so on counting backwards. When you lose your place, which is inevitable if you are breathing slowly, just start all over. This is meditation.

Meditation can be daydreaming. It can just be sitting quietly "catching and being aware" of all of the thoughts running through your head. Meditation can be sitting out in nature closing your eyes and noticing all the different sounds you hear. It can be holding a rock or flower and noticing everything you can about it. Meditation is about learning to focus the thoughts. It is all about gaining control of your brain and the thoughts that are generated. Try letting everything go and rest your thoughts. Relax. Feel what is happening in your body. Wonderful new solutions and ideas can spring forth when you let your thoughts relax. This is why meditation is so helpful.

I want you to replace outdated ruts in your brain with ones that will create the life you want to live. It takes practice. Be patient and kind with yourself as you change old ruts. It is like learning to breath in a healthier way. It took me years of practicing healthier breathing for it to become second nature.

I was a chest breather. Our abdominal organs love to be massaged and oxygenated with each breath. When you inhale let the belly expand first. Take the breath all the way to the bottom floor below your waistline. Learn to pause for a couple seconds before letting your breath out. Let the breath leave your belly collapsing and the air from your lungs leaving last. Some prefer to let the exhale come out through their open mouth like blowing out a candle. Others prefer to exhale through the nasal passage. Choose what works for you and be open to changing that at any later time. Then pause another couple seconds before inhaling again.

When you find yourself stressed, overly excited, starting a panic attack, getting an uncontrollable emotion rising like anger, take a few slow conscious deep breaths before doing anything. First this exercise causes you to become more aware of your emotions as they rise within you. You will be able to catch the emotion and make a choice to have a different response. You will start being in control of your thoughts and not letting your brain be a runaway and in control of you.

After all, that uncontrollable anger and yelling at your partner may just be a result of them having an expression or behavior that reminds you of when you were little, and you were unable to defend yourself in an argument that was unfair. Maybe your parent would get that expression or stance before they slapped you for no reason. It is just a trigger that is yet unidentified in you that causes you to go on automatic behavior. That is why I want to help you notice your emotions. They are the gold nuggets of getting the life you really want to be living.

Another tool in healing is remembering how to play and have fun. Return to being a child and really play with your partner or others in your life. There are no rules as long as you are safe and considerate of others. We are way too serious. I was just told by a man that was transferred here from Dubai, who has lived and worked in many countries around the globe, that he finds Americans to be unhappy and that they eat way too fast. He said they go to work, go home and go to work, just repeating the cycle. Take a moment and play! Have fun! It is ok and is necessary for good health.

Just as much as playing is necessary for good health, so is rest and sleep. I notice so often how our brains are programmed by others. For example most of us believe we need about eight hours of sleep to be healthy. This is really absurd in my opinion. Remember how I have stressed that everyone is different and unique?

Some people may require ten hours of sleep every night and others only require three. I have heard people that only require three or four hours a night state they know that is unhealthy and they will pay for it. They mean they will get sick eventually, and they will because they believe they will. However, these individuals look healthy and function quite alertly. Why can't these people trust their own bodies and be in touch with their body? Maybe this year they only need four hours of sleep and in a few years they will only require two hours or maybe twelve. Learn to be open to what is. We must learn our own unique body, and believe in it, and honor what it needs regardless of what someone else believes. Please program your own brain with your own software that is true for you.

The person that only sleeps four hours at night may be a person that takes short naps or may not. Whatever makes that person healthy is right for them. Rest and sleep are necessary for the human body but only in the amounts that your body needs. If you listen to your body you will know what it needs. The needs of your body changes each day, or may remain constant for years. Just listen to your body is all that I am asking, without using any unconscious programmed beliefs about what is right for you, that has been put in your software by others.

A good affirmation for this would be, I always know what is right for me. Please remember if using affirmations, that it is imperative that you word them correctly. They are an excellent tool in helping you to heal. Word them as though you have already attained what you want. Results will not come quickly if you start your affirmations with: I am not, or I can be, or I will be, or I am becoming.

In order for an affirmation to be a healing tool, you must make a statement claiming something as though you already have it. Use words like I am and I have. I also suggest saying I am a joyful, calm, and centered person instead of saying I am free of anger. I do not want your affirmations having any low vibrational words in them.

I want you to repeat your affirmations out loud. This is very important! Even better is to say them out loud in front of a mirror. Be that Emmy award winning actor. Play the part you want to achieve. You need to feel it in every molecule of your body with joy and meaning. It needs to light you up when you repeat it. Feel it with emotion when you say it. If it doesn't make you feel good, you have some unconscious thoughts running that are contradicting the affirmation, and you will not get the change you want. To practice saying the affirmations with good feeling emotion is much more important than the number of times that you repeat them daily.

It is a choice whether you continue repeating your affirmations until they no longer feel awkward and wrong when you say them. WE ALWAYS HAVE A CHOICE. This is a very important tool in your healing. No matter what, we always have a choice. We may think we don't have a choice, but that is created by an underlying belief we have and it is playing the victim role. If we could remove that filter of "there is no choice in this situation" we would see several, maybe even endless choices that we could make.

Here again, I have great compassion for people who don't think they have a choice. I was literally in my early fifties before I understood that I had a choice in every situation and of course I am still working on changing this rut. It took me awhile to understand and learn that I was playing the victim role, and not being the Creator in my life when I would tell myself I did not have a choice. I had to do such and such.

Remember it is always better to make a decision and get energy and life flowing, than to get stuck in I don't know what to do, which is similar to saying, I don't have a choice in this matter. Saying to yourself that you do not know is literally playing victim, and not being the Warrior you are. Nothing will happen when you repeat I don't know what to do. Say instead that I am open to ideas of what I can do.

We are on the planet of learning lessons, which means that we will never get it all done and we cannot get it wrong. Whatever decision you make, you will learn from it. So keep moving, by making a decision and taking action.

Life is like floating down the river. Would you absolutely put down anchor to keep from moving forward and try resisting the flow? Would you insist on paddling upstream against the strong current? Isn't that what you do when you stay in indecision, mulling and mulling over what to do? Isn't that what you are doing when you forcefully control and exert your preferences on the outcome of a situation? Don't put off until tomorrow what you can do today.

Imagine we are all walking a path that leads us to the farthest distant galaxy outside of the Milky Way, which we believe is impossible to do. Also know that the Universe is forever growing and expanding. See that our road is so long, it really doesn't matter how fast we try to get to the end, because it is ever expanding and we can never ever reach the end of it. We are all at different places on the path. The end of the path doesn't exist, because it is growing longer as we walk on it. As they say, stop and smell the roses! What is your hurry? Savor the moment. It is the journey that matters, not the destination!

Call 100% of your Spirit back to you and be a Warrior. Quit giving up your power to others. Whenever you go after or want a person, place or thing because you believe it will make you happy; you are giving up your power to that person, place or thing. I told this to a dear friend of mine who thought she couldn't go on because her partner had left her. Be a Warrior that is solid and can stand alone, without being dependent on other people or possessing objects.

When you are not shyly or overtly strutting your peacock feathers you are not walking in your power. You are standing in your power when you know whatever anyone says or does will not, or cannot harm you, or take away your happiness and joy. Stop defending yourself and just stand quietly in your power. When you respond no to someone, you are not required to give any explanations. Stand quietly in your power of no. We make excuses so we don't face and take care of what needs to be done or dealt with. Please do today what you can. Don't put it off until tomorrow. Why make tomorrow's list longer?

Successful Life Muffin Recipe

By: Doctor of Life

14 lbs of Warming Self Love

7 sticks of straight posture

7 bags of healthy breathing

7 bags of play and exercise

7 bags of sleep and rest

7 bags of happy fulfilling work

1 to 28 bags of playful sexual satisfaction

14 bags of intentional positive thoughts

7 bags of light-hearted self examination

Topping:

7 lbs of Self praise for a life well lived

14 lbs of Love

Before lightly tossing the first nine ingredients together, and setting aside in a large bowl, the cook must prepare themselves. Take a deep breath, get present, and set the intent to make the muffins with total and complete love. Now gently toss the first nine ingredients when you are ready. Too much stirring makes for a tough muffin.

Thoughtfully, gently, and thoroughly stir together the two topping ingredients sending lots of love into each gentle stir.

Gently divide the ingredients into 7 well loved muffin tins and cover with topping, being sure to use all batter and topping mix.

Doctor of Life suggests taking 15 minutes to consume one muffin daily, early in the morning while sitting down without any electronic device, cell phone, TV, iPad, iPod, radio, music, newspaper, magazine, book, or other distractions going on. Love you body enough to give it attention and time to eat.

The Dr. recommends sitting in nature, or watching nature out the window, or admiring a real flower, or watching a candle burn on the table while consuming your muffin. The Dr. asks that you silently or out loud thank and be grateful to all who made this muffin possible to be in front of you.

The Dr. insists on you taking a deep slow breath before EACH and EVERY bite which helps you notice, think about, and focus on the delicious taste, smell, texture, color, and sound of each bite of the muffin.

The Dr. says to chew each bite thoroughly and completely before swallowing. Do not put another bite into your mouth, until you swallow the previous bite. The Dr. says it is imperative that you follow this instruction. Ok everyone, this means only one peanut M&M at a time in your mouth. Not a handful all at once!

He wants you to also believe that your body's intelligence will only take from each bite exactly what it needs for excellent health, nothing more and nothing less. Anything else will just pass on through your body unused. Really savor and enjoy the bites.

Sit for 4-5 minutes quietly and consciously breathing after the muffin is completed to give your body a few moments to process and start digestion, before going to your next activity. Dr. Life says this shows some self respect and love to yourself and your body.

Another tool follows that is outlined in a different way.

BALANCE – INTENT – THE DAILY BASICS

PHYSICAL – Learn to breathe correctly, relax and have good posture.

- Learn and practice correct posture.
- Chin and shoulders down
- Shoulders back and chest out

- Strengthen your muscles-nothing is more important to a healthy fun life
- Learn and practice correct breathing
- Plenty of rest and sleep
- Good quality food and water

EMOTIONAL – Look at yourself daily in the mirror and say I love you and you are wonderful!

- Notice your emotions as they occur. Ask what am I feeling?
- Identify your emotions
- Learn to be in charge of your emotions and not allow your emotions to have control over you
- Know that any emotions you feel are all about you, not the other person.

MENTAL – Ask yourself what did I just say? Learn how and practice cleaning your filters.

- Learn brain control. Control your computer.
- Learn how and program your brain's software---the beliefs and thoughts you have
- Learn your life is a projection of how you treat yourself, and that you can change it

SPIRITUAL –Ask yourself what did I just hear?

- Learn what your beliefs are.
- Start meditating daily…..many many ways of achieving this
- Learn and start "hearing" your inner self when it speaks
- Become your inner jewel

Yet another tool for you is to have a Mr. Match in your life. Mr. Match is a recent man that has entered my life that really puts me on alert. He has gifts he doesn't realize at all that he has. This is one of my gifts. The ability to see what others possess inside of them and what their obstacles are that are keeping them from their gifts. He sees and knows all. He has studied people and knows how to get what he wants, sometimes to his own demise. Yes, he is a "trained' salesman. But deeper than that he has a heart and moral system that he follows even if others disagree. I have no masks or walls of defense when I am with him. He calls me on all of them. I am also able to call him on his, which makes for a wonderful relationship.

He's going to be a fun ride while forcing me to face my demons and blocks all the while having fun and being pushed out of my comfort zone continually. Things I feel at ease and comfortable with others, I feel tense and uptight doing with him because I know I'm not hidden from his gaze. It's unnerving to have met your match. I'm a smartass, well yes, I am sometimes, and he matches me even on that. This will be a real learning curve for me with him. I only hope you have or will have a Mr. Match in your life someday with the agreement of helping each other grow.

I cannot end the chapter on tools without re-emphasizing, that the most important advice I can give you is to continue to look yourself in the eye, in the mirror, each and every day, and say I love you with meaning and emotion. I cried when I looked at myself in the eye for the first time. It took me a long time to get to the point where I could say I love you Kathy and really feel like there was some real love emotion in the statement.

Several of my clients have the same issue and I have to keep reminding them to do it each and every day. It must be repeated to become a rut and automatic in your brain. Get a picture of yourself that you admire, no matter what age you were, and lovingly frame it and put the words I love you on it. Leave it in your bedroom or bathroom or wherever you will see it often daily. I cannot stress enough how this one, and only one daily habit will totally transform your life. Just try it. You have everything to gain. What do you have to lose? It's just a few seconds every day!

CHAPTER 6 - FOOD FOR THOUGHT with Mr. Wonder

Ohhhh…..when we met, we both felt the total prior life attachment. Mr. Wonder was a Pisces and very young. He was tall, lean, handsome, alluring and looking into his eyes I saw the playful child followed by the very old wise soul. We knew each other and were connected just like Mr. Renaissance and I were. It was a whirlwind romance where we were very meaningfully connected and explored many new areas.

He was such an old wise soul, here on Earth once again, to go through the process of revealing his own gifts and then to help others. He and I found total fun, joy, and connection together. Our age difference did not matter and only gave us another reason to play and joke around. We felt so comfortable together and we could say anything to each other without reserve, knowing that the other would not abandon us over something we felt and needed to say. We respected each other.

We have so much in common and so many ways of helping each other. We are like an old married couple. He has been a gem and savior for me. He kept me sane and here when I didn't think I could take anymore. He reintroduced me to the bubble bath and so many other beautiful ways of loving myself. He kept me laughing. He'd say if you want to do it or try it, let's do it.

Mr. Wonder had a traumatic childhood like most of us. It is an ongoing process for him to heal the beliefs controlling his life today. However, he moves relentlessly forward so that he can reveal his own jewels inside of him. Parents do not realize what a strong effect they have upon their children. They impose beliefs on their children that they are not even conscious of. The parents are usually still in the midst of trying to heal themselves when they have children.

Let us talk about our children now. As parents and adults, you are the children's example. They learn and do from your actions, not your words. Please reread that if you haven't thought about the beliefs you have programmed in your brain on this subject. Is hitting a child how you choose to teach them? Or are you repeating what was done to you without questioning the beliefs underlying the actions? Do you believe spare the rod spoil the child? You are going to teach by hitting or slapping your child? Do we want the teachers, mentors, and employers hitting and slapping our children to teach them how to learn?

What is a spoiled child? Is a spoiled child one that has had no consistent boundaries set for them? They want what they want when they want it, or they get loud and active. Is the parent guilty of saying one time they can't have candy in the checkout lane and giving in to their begging on another day. What is the child to believe? They will test the water and see what will happen. If however, the child knows repeatedly that over and over they never get candy in the checkout lane they will quit asking. It even helps a lot more for them to be educated on the good rational foundational reasons why you don't want them having candy in the checkout lane. They can then learn how to make good decisions and set boundaries for themselves as they grow older.

We need to teach our children healthy self awareness, self discipline, healthy boundaries, self esteem, self confidence, etc. Children will behave, learn and feel good about themselves when they are respected and taught how to feel good about themselves. They learn a lot about this by watching how their parents love themselves or abuse themselves.

We do not need to teach them to stay in an unhealthy, unhappy, loveless, self demeaning, relationship for the sake of the children. Your children know a lot more than you give them credit for. Children always know when their parents are unhappy. They know every emotion you are feeling; no matter how well you think you are hiding it from them. They learn by your actions. They also know at that point, that you are not being truthful with them. Trust cannot be built when people are not truthful with each other. They will grow up learning to hide, stuff, and discount what they are really feeling because you have taught them to.

Children feel the energy moving between people. We all do, but many of us have discounted, ignored and buried our ability to feel it. However, I am sure you have walked in on someone, and without words being spoken, you know they are angry or happy or very sad. You feel the energy emanating from their body's energy field.

We do not need to try and live our life through our children. They came with their own purpose to fulfill and their own inner treasure chest of gifts. Who are we to control and try to change their life's desires? Did you like someone telling you what to do with your life? Support and encourage them in what they want to do. Parents so often will try and get their children to do something they missed out on, or didn't chose to do, or their dream they haven't lived. That is the parent's issue and not your child's, who has their very own agenda for life.

How many people do you know that became successful or unsuccessful in careers that they really didn't want to do? They did not choose their career. They let someone else choose it for them. They accepted everyone else's software programming for their brain and didn't become the artist or musician or designer because they knew they could not make a living doing that. I have met so many people in this situation and they are sometimes so very blind to it. Their programming ruts are deeper than the Grand Canyon in their brains.

I suggest you work on yourself and set a good learning example for your children. If you cannot do this, then go learn how to do it for yourself and your children. Don't mess up their lives. Go straighten out yours. That is the best learning and teaching example you could ever give your child. Remember it is never about the other person, it is all about you. Maybe it is time to go feel, catch and excavate again?

We really do not want to have control over our children in the sense of what they do for their careers and big life decisions. If you are trying to control their life and plans, it is because you are not tending to your own business and are using them as a distraction from doing your own work. I had to learn to let go of control. Of course, I'm still working on this one, but the Universe gave me some pretty intense lessons to help me. This included control of everything, including other people. Of course I would have said I didn't try to control other people, but I did and I believe most people do. We all have an agenda and we want it to go our way and we have very subtle ways of achieving our means. These may very well be unconscious to us, but it is our job to bring those actions up to consciousness and heal them.

If you are in a relationship and the other person wants out, then we need to bless them and wish them happiness in their journey. Be grateful for the time we had with them. Who wants to live with somebody that doesn't want to be with them? Freely let them go. Forgive them for not being able to honor your agreement, if in fact you did discuss and make an agreement. Maybe some of you need to think about discussing what your agreement is rather than assuming what it is.

Our happiness is not dependent upon our partner or anyone else. We are responsible for our own happiness. Set the example for all the people you are connected with on how to be authentic and responsible for your own life. When you heal and act differently, the people around you will also heal, change or leave. You are creating a new life from the new beliefs, thoughts, and emotions you are now having. Change must occur.

What better way is there to try and control people than to make them sad, hopeless, guilty, depressed, wrong and sinful? Isn't this the case of seeing what is wrong in the moment rather than what is right in the moment? What if you were given these beliefs and rules to live by that said you must forever live with the same partner, must never steal, must never kill, must not want or have desires, and must always stop at stop signs.

What would you do if someone was ready to kill your loved ones? Would you kill in self defense? What would you do if your loved ones were starving? Would you steal food? If you were out in flat open countryside where you could see for miles, and there was no other car, would you stop at the stop sign? Is life only black and white, or are there many shades of gray in between? Are there always exceptions and rationalizations to every rule?

Rationalization and defending our opinions is very tricky. We all use it to make ourselves right. No one wants to be wrong. We use rationalization to suit us and our desires. Mr. Wonder always points out to me when I go into defense mode.

What is your reaction to being called sweetheart, slut, sexy, bastard, my love, son of a bitch, sweetie, whore, sugar daddy, prostitute, doll-baby, and bitch? Words are language. Words can be used with intent and emotion…..i.e. energy. May I suggest maybe you have some deep ruts on some of these words that play before you even know what is going on? Did these words cause emotion in you? Mr. Wonder was always saying I wonder what is underlying that, when I would start showing emotions of defensiveness.

Mr. Wonder and I would have many conversations about society and how customs and trends with people and families have changed over the decades. I will always remember my mother-in-law and the many things I learned from her.

She never had a pile of dirty dishes after she cooked. I observed her as she would wash and put away everything when she was done with it. It actually added very little time to the preparation but saved tons of time during clean up. She was an expert organizer and planner. She knew exactly when she was completely finished with a bowl or spoon, and would then wash it and put it away.

I only discovered how excellent she was in this area when I tried doing it her way. I found myself getting that same washed item back out again. I did learn as I practiced, and still to this day incorporate her process when I am cooking. This was no doubt part of her inner jewel that I don't believe she ever really fully revealed or maybe discovered.

She made the best chicken and dumplings, and her kitchen was clean as she put the last dumpling in the pot to be cooked. I really admired her talent and have always been grateful for learning this from her. I try and have no regrets, but I do wish I had expressed to her how very much I appreciated learning this from her. I forget sometimes that the smallest, most insignificant compliments and praise can be the most meaningful to the recipient.

In my opinion any male or female that truly and successfully runs the household, while raising young children at the same time, are among the most talented, organized, problem solving, creative people among us. Especially the ones that are happy doing it.

It takes excellent top rate ingenuity to keep the house clean, the meals cooked, groceries bought, laundry completed, bills paid, children clean and fed, and all this completed during the hours that the other partner is at work. That way everyone can be together during the evening at dinner relaxing, playing, and enjoying one another.

Children's bedtime is around 8pm leaving a couple of hours for the partners to enjoy alone time together. This is definitely a fading dissolving job as our society goes forward, but is still held in our collective unconscious. This is not to be confused with the Stepford wives or is it?

It just seems I see the pendulum swinging maybe too far when the job paying working partner is expected to do more and more household jobs. This is because the other partner runs the children to all sorts of activities, gets manicures and pedicures, salon treatments, does lots of shopping, social gatherings and then complains about too much to do. Where is our balance in this lifestyle? Are the babies enjoying the activities or really just being over stimulated? Are the mothers trying to live a life they feel they missed through their child? Is it a rationalization to say I really love my child and want to provide him or her with every opportunity? Maybe in reality loving the child would be giving them some down time and really listening to what they say they want to do. Maybe all the activity is to avoid feeling emotions. Loving our self would be having time to feel.

I am not saying which man, but one of my men asked me how do I love myself? We love ourselves like we would love our child or loved one. When an innocent vulnerable infant needs food because they are hungry, we feed them right then. When they need a nap or to go to bed for the night, we let them. When they want to play and interact we play with them with total presence. We hug and kiss them with real emotion of love.

When our children want too much of something or physically act out where it hurts others, we set boundaries for them. Just like setting boundaries for our self so we don't over indulge in any one thing. I believe the word here, would be addiction. We need balance in everything! When your child really wants or needs something we do our best to provide it for them. We need to do no less for ourselves if we truly are loving ourselves.

When you are asked who is first on your priority list it needs to be you! Remember we cannot honestly give to others what we do not give to and have an excess of ourselves. We have to learn to eat healthy when we are hungry. We need to rest and sleep when we are tired. We need to play and have fun to stay in balance. Equal amounts of work, play and rest are required by healthy balanced individuals.

There are no arguments or rationalizations against loving yourself that hold any validity in my opinion. Life flows easily when we unconditionally love ourselves and integrate that fully into every cell and way of being within us. We believe we are truly worthy of our own love, and that we are important enough to give our self the things we really need and want.

This means saying No when you need to. I want especially the women, men, mothers, and fathers that need to hear this understand that when you say no, you do not give an explanation, you do not go into excuses, and you say no more words, unless you choose to repeat "no" as your answer. There is a time and place to help children understand why the answer is no, but do not fall into their manipulation and games by starting to discuss the issue. You may lose. You will nearly always lose to a child and a good salesman. The answer is no. They learn from how you act. Help them learn that no means no. Respect yourself and then other people will respect you.

When there is an important fund raiser and you are asked to provide home baked cookies, but you are dog tired, you say No and take care of yourself. When your spouse or society tells you how to wear your hair, what clothes to wear, and it really goes against the core of your personality you say no. When the salesman won't respect you and take no for an answer, and starts talking about emotion, you need to walk away because he is going for the hard sale to convince you to say yes. An old school salesman has learned how to manipulate people into getting the sale he wants with whatever it takes. We need to learn to stand in our power and not be manipulated by others.

Living our life by others' expectations of us is selling our self out. We are not honoring and loving ourselves, and we are enabling others to be in someone's business other than their own. They are trying to exert control upon us and their external life. The only place we have any business exerting control is within ourselves. We only do it to others because they allow us to, and it gives us a false sense of being in control when in fact, it shows how out of control we really are. The only way we change this is by getting out of other people's lives and getting fully into our own.

It means accepting the responsibility that I am the only one responsible for me, and how I behave, and live my life. No one makes me angry or sad or helpless. I choose to feel that way. I may feel an emotion from their behavior but it is ONLY my filter and beliefs that determine what I do with that emotion. Either I react and blame them, living externally as an outside force, or I go within and dissect the beliefs and thoughts underlying my emotion living internally.

My hope for us is that we chose to consciously start living internally. We will fall asleep and wake up repeating I love you (your name) and smiling as we say it. We will feel the warmth and energy from our heart radiate throughout our body. As we stand in front of the mirror we will look our self in the eyes and say I love you (our name) and feel that warmth flood through our body. We will hug our self and start hugging others. Humans need physical touch and to deny ourselves of that is not loving our self.

May we start resting and sleeping when our body needs it. We will learn to live internally and recognize hunger pains, tiredness, and the need for play and fun. We will give to our self what we are needing and wanting. We will live by our very own internal code of ethics.

We will be true to our self and not deceive our self anymore. May we think carefully before making a promise to our self that we might not keep? We will start keeping promises we do make to our self and others. If we still want that hat with the feather in it, we will go get it for our self. We will wear it happily and free of guilt as long as it wasn't bought through an addiction. If we really want to take dance lessons, we will work it out so we can, whether our partner compromises and wants us to or not. We will pay attention to and follow our inner most treasured desires. We will live by our own internal expectations and not by outside external expectations of us.

Know there are consequences and reactions for every action we take on Earth. So consider that in our choices, but do not let it keep us from being true to our self. We will give up abusing our self by believing the job will never get done, or get done right if we don't do it our self, if we don't do it now, if we don't hurry up, if we don't work hard and push our self. We will learn how to receive and how to ask for help when we need it. That was not an easy lesson for me by the way.

May we no longer sell out our code of ethics and work for a company whose policies and practices we do not support and cannot live with. If we would all follow our hearts more, the companies would have to change their policies because they would dissolve and cease to exist. Do we feel good up selling and manipulating a customer, high pressure closing and selling of unneeded items just because we've been told it is our job? We've been taught how to manipulate people by their emotions, using fear based selling and debt collecting, and selling with lies. These would all vanish if we lived from our hearts and refused to do it. We need to reexamine living for the dollar. Employees are enabling the company and entity to exist and continue with lower principals and ethics, because they are not internally living and loving themselves by standing up and saying, no longer will I do that. What were all the people doing that followed Hitler?

Our external world we live in is ONLY and totally uniquely ONLY a reflection of how the masses are living internally. Let's change the world!!!

Men are taught they are not a man if they express their emotions. Men are told to be strong, protect, provide for others, and act like a man at all costs to themselves. Men learn to ignore their feelings in order to be a man. They believe they have to be tough at the expense of having a heart and feeling.

Women are taught to care for everyone else and forsake and ignore themselves in doing so. Women are taught they are responsible for how everyone behaves and feels which is total insanity.

We all long for strong emotional deep love with another human being. We feel we need to be wanted. This is because we are not giving the love to our self and we look for it externally. We attach externally to someone and allow ourselves to feel devastated, unloved, and unworthy again when that person treats us badly. Maybe they appear through our filter to be unappreciative when we cook their meal, do their work, come to their rescue and give them a break from life, when they are not feeling well or we just want to. Yet all they do is say what is wrong, and complain, and correct everything we did. They tell us what else we should have done to really show we loved them. We use drama to control others.

I feel this is a self abusive fulfilling cycle we are in. We prefer to stay in brain ruts of self abuse because sometimes it's the only "love" we've ever known in life. We keep recreating it, hoping it will suddenly fulfill our yearning for that deep loving emotional bond we so desperately want to feel. Remember the ego makes us all feel "separate" when in reality we are all very connected. We all share and breathe the same atoms of life.

In my opinion I feel that we are only enabling an abuser to continue abusing. We are being an abuser to our self for allowing someone to treat us that way. They are also probably continuing the abusive behavior they saw modeled to them and are probably doing it unconsciously. However, we are also enabling them as an abuser by allowing our self to be the recipient of their actions. Where would they be if not one of us allowed ourselves to be treated that way?

When we really start internally integrating loving our self; that type of person will no longer be able to exist in our external world!!!

Thank the Universe for our gay people. They are our frontiersmen and women for living true to their inner self and what they need. The gay people I have met are the most loving and emotionally open people I've ever encountered. Lots of the gay people still don't unconditionally love themselves, but I have to applaud them for starting to meet their internal desires. Remember we never get it all done, and there is no finish line, and there is no right or wrong way. Earth is a place of contrast and learning lessons. We may come back another lifetime and deal with the same issue again, but just make a different choice to see what happens that way. It's like a big real life strategy game.

Let's talk about love. First, let me state that we cannot give what we don't have or give our self. This means if we do not truly unconditionally love our self then we cannot truly love someone else. That probably raised some emotion. That is good. Follow it back to its source.

When we look at a photograph of our self do we see all of our good qualities? That means do we see what is right in the moment? I'm so pretty, so happy, I look good. OR when we look at a photograph of our self do we see everything that is wrong? Oh, I look awful, I'm not smiling, my hair is a mess, get rid of that picture, I'm so fat, that is my bad side, etc., etc.

Better yet for some of us, will we even let people take our photograph? Do we hide from the camera? Do we absolutely refuse to have our picture taken? If so, what does that say to our body? I don't like you, I'm not proud of you, I'm ashamed of you. These are all signs of whether we love our self or we don't love our self.

I have one more example of loving yourself. Can we look at our self in the eye in the mirror and say "I love you."? I challenge you to get into character and look every morning and every night in the mirror at yourself and say I love you and you are beautiful, out loud to yourself! Now for some of you this may seem impossible or just hard but I guarantee you, it will change your life! Start looking at your partner, your friends in the eye and saying it with the same meaning and emotion. Just be a Warrior and DO IT!......everyday......it has to be a ongoing cumulative effort to fill in that deep brain rut that swallows cars whole.

We must learn to accept ourselves just as we are. We must forgive ourselves. We cannot truly forgive someone else until we can forgive ourselves. We must know that we have been good and bad. All of us have been good and bad. We have lots of experiences in life to learn and grow. Maybe reading The Little Soul and the Sun by Neale Donald Walsch might help some of you. Maybe watching the movie Predestination will make you think. Maybe the following rules will make you think.

RULES FOR BEING HUMAN

1. You will receive a body. You may like it or hate it, but it will be yours for the entire period this time around.

2. You will learn lessons. You are enrolled in a full-time informal school called life. Each day in this school you will have the opportunity to learn lessons. You may like the lessons or think them irrelevant and stupid.

3. There are no mistakes, only lessons. Growth is a process of trial and error and experimentation. The "failed" experiments are as much a part of the process as the experiment that ultimately "works".

4. A lesson is repeated until learned. A lesson will be presented to you in various forms until you have learned it. When you have learned it, you can then go on to the next lesson.

5. Learning lessons does not end. There is no part of life that does not contain its lessons. If you are alive, there are lessons to be learned.

6. "There" is no better place than "here". When your "there" has become a "here", you will simply obtain another "there" that will again, look better than "here".

7. Others are merely mirrors of you. You cannot love or hate something about another person unless it reflects to you something you love or hate about yourself.

8. What you make of your life is up to you. You have all the tools and resources you need. What you do with them is up to you. The choice is yours.

9. Your answers lie inside you. The answers to life's questions lie inside you. All you need to do is look, listen, and trust.

10. You will forget all this.

Author unknown

Found on a refrigerator

In Toronto

These rules for being human made me stop in my tracks and think when I first came across them in a fellow worker's office in the early 2000's. I asked him if I could copy it and I have referred to it many times. I 'know" inside of me that it speaks the truth about life, because of the way is resonates with me each and every time I read it.

Heaven and Hell are here on Earth created by each of us. We must live in reverence of all living things, be it Mother Earth, the plant, animal, or insect kingdoms. Are rocks alive? Be open-minded; be willing to explore unknown horizons like the ones that believed the Earth was not flat. (Do I need to remind you to feel the emotions that just rose? And to catch the thoughts racing through your brain, and excavate the underlying beliefs for that entire reaction you just felt? Your emotions are your key to healing!)

Think about these statements. Our lock on ourselves is what other people think of us. Please reread that statement. Our lock on ourselves is what other people think of us. Free your inhibitions, put the key in that lock, and unlock yourself. You don't care, or more importantly you don't live your life by what others think. Live your life by your very own inner moral code that resides inside of you.

CHAPTER 7 - MY STORY with Mr. Columbian

You will also need a Mr. Columbian, a Pisces. He spotted me on a very short lived dating site I was on and asked me for a drink. I decided to go. After all, he was cute. Am I ever glad I took that chance? You bet I am.

Actually he was strong, dominant, muscular and very good looking. He was the quiet type. His accent made it difficult for me to understand him at times; the same way he had trouble with my accent. He's what I'd say gently dominant and full of surprises. He has shocked me with his expertise and variety of experiences. He is gentle and yet very rugged. He is a total joy.

He appears from the dark enchanted jungle right when I need him without question. He walks through my door and takes me on the spot gently and smoothly. He leans me against the wall as he gently turns my face toward him by firmly pulling the hair on the back of my head. After slowly undressing me and kissing me all over, he returns to my mouth, he gazes for a long time into my eyes and then picks me up. He places me on the countertop island in the kitchen, lays me down and explores me more fully. Later he picks me up and carries me to the bed. He is total ecstasy. Afterwards he always disappears like a misty fog back into the jungle, until the next time I desire him. I miss him every day he doesn't visit me.

Now I am going to tell you a story about his partner Ms. Warrior, an Aries female, and about part of her life journey. She also whimsically appears like a fog from the enchanted jungle. She is me, the author of this book. Please remember that our life journey is always ongoing. It is never finished. This is but a segment of my life. In 2003, after years of restlessness, discontent, yearning, sadness, feeling alone, unwanted, unworthy, not belonging and displaced, but looking perfect and happy to others, I knew something had to change in my life.

On January 18, 2003, on the full moon I sent out the following request to the Universe. I had to have more from life. I wanted to know, help and feel fulfillment and satisfaction from helping thousands of people discover their inner treasures and dreams. I wanted to actually help them live their dreams without ever leaving my farm. I had my request written on a torn sheet of paper that laid on my dresser and I read it often.

A year later on January 18, 2004, the Universe gifted me with the opportunity to capture a once in a lifetime picture of the sun rising. It looked perfectly like a cross in the sky. I can vividly remember feeling the excitement and shaking in my body that I felt that day, when I took the picture. Every time I tell the story of taking the picture, it's like I am back in that very moment reliving it. It occurred in slow motion. I remember everything I did and everything I felt. I knew deep inside of me that somehow that picture was very important to me. I tried figuring it out, but nothing ever came to fruition. Little did I know what symbolic meaning this had and what the Universe had planned for me.

On January 19, 2005, I was exposed to a cleaning chemical at work in an office building that was over one hundred years old, and that changed my life forever. I had to leave work that day and spent the next four days in bed feeling like the worst flu ever had taken me over. Within two weeks of the exposure I had to quit working, because I was having trouble breathing around perfumes and dry cleaned suits. Something was happening to my brain, and I was not able to do my accounting work.

Within four weeks I could no longer drive, and I was deteriorating fast. My washer, dryer, phone and computer made me feel very strange, weak, shaky and very sick using them. I was having more trouble breathing and my heart would race. I found a doctor in St. Louis and saw him daily for the last two weeks of February 2005.

On the last day of February 2005 I had my first two seizures in that doctor's office. He arranged for me to see a doctor in Dallas. I was "overnighted" by car because I couldn't fly from Southern Illinois, my home, and arrived in Dallas, Texas on March 1, 2005. I could not return to southern Illinois because of mold issues there and have remained in Dallas ever since.

Within six weeks of the chemical exposure, I went from a fully functioning Accountant Supervisor to having four to six seizures a day that lasted sixty to ninety minutes each. I was unable to walk by myself, feed myself, go to the bathroom by myself or dress myself. I had heard nothing about environmental illness, other than I had seen the 1976 John Travolta movie "The Boy in the Plastic Bubble" which also dealt with a deficient immune system, and was very similar to my condition in many ways. Nor had I ever heard anything about an Electromagnetic Frequency Illness.

I began my seven year journey of transforming myself into a healthier person by healing myself totally from an Environmental Illness (E.I.) coupled with an Electro Magnetic Frequency (EMF) Illness. I was literally allergic and sensitive to most everything and had to live in the least toxic environment I could find. I learned many things on this journey.

In the fall of 2005, I had two medical doctors tell me I would have died under their care. I also had another medical doctor tell me there was nothing more they could do for me at my lowest time. I would be dead and this book would not have been written by me if not for my determination, my Warrior spirit and the help of some very caring people. My condition could not be healed, abated, or covered up with medication by regular medical doctors. With the support of my loved ones, the medical community, the body energy healer and workers, and my counselor I was able to conquer the illnesses.

I continued to have four to six seizures that were ninety minutes long each and every day. I called them my aerobic workouts. Yes, somehow I was able to retain some humor. I couldn't speak or hear during the seizures. I had uncontrolled violent shaking of the right side of my body. My hair and clothes were soaked with sweat after the seizures. I was starved afterwards. Finally I had to have a person on each side of me to be able to walk. I refused a wheelchair. We all set our limits as to how far we will go, even in illness.

Little did I know what was yet to come. There were EMF problems that caused the car's turn signal, buzzers, and windshield wipers to set off my seizures. So did cell phones, refrigerators running, sirens, batteries, computers, all electrical items, and power plants within two blocks of me. The body pain was so intense it felt like being hit by a fleet of Mack trucks or being trampled by a stadium full of people and at the same time having electrical current run through my body 24/7. It took me twenty minutes to walk with assistance up thirty steps to my room. I was living in an almost sterile environment, wearing a face mask anytime I was outside of my room, unable to go shopping, unable to have visitors, unable to ride in anyone's car but my own safe one. I could not be driven over twenty-five miles per hour in my car without it causing a seizure. I felt Hurricane Katrina totally unbalance and unsettle my body while I resided in Dallas, Texas.

I made one large mistake and missed buying stock in Kleenex. My excuse was I was too sick, but it was really my fear of not enough money. I cried so many many healing tears and continue to do so, but on a much less frequent basis now. By the way, I was such a consumer back then, that I noticed immediately when they reduced the size of a Kleenex. I always wondered why the box didn't smile and say I love you with a kiss every time I pulled a Kleenex from it. Or maybe a baby giggle could have been played to raise my vibrational frequency and help me get well. I have lots of invention ideas that I keep written in a special book, hoping one day to bring them to development.

It was taking five to fifteen minutes to just get my body out of bed because of the aches and pains. Oh yes, I just remembered the airplanes also set off my seizures during the early days. I could tell you if it was a helicopter, big jet, or small plane before you could hear or see it. Yes, I know this sounds like a science fiction person but it is true, every word of it. After the seizures slowed down from the body energy work, the airplanes just unbalanced and wrecked my body for a few years. My senses were all at such an extreme high sensitivity level that it was unheard of, and people have a hard time believing it.

I could predict up to forty-eight hours before a storm hit. I would have a huge appetite increase, felt very unbalanced, unsettled, depressed and had extreme tiredness that would make me literally crumble and lay down. During the storm, I could tell you if the lightning was cloud to cloud or cloud to ground by the feel of it without even seeing it. I felt lightning shatter my body for many miles away, when you could not even hear the thunder.

I had to detox everything I used or bought. That is a huge process and time consumer that I will not go into here. I was on the rotation all organic diet and drank only glass bottled spring water. My severe headaches and extreme shooting head pain on the right side of my brain was constant daily and lasted for over two years. After that it was still very frequent, but today I am pain free. I studied and learned by myself about pain in my body and how to live with it. I was unable to take any prescription medications, over the counter drugs, supplements, or herbs.

I spent hours and hours and days and months and years of pain and healing tears doing the emotional, mental, and spiritual work that was needed, and was guided by a very dedicated energy healer and my counselor. Some part of me inside knew this was necessary, even though it was the most challenging thing I'd ever done. Yes, there were many times I wanted to quit.

I was so thankful for my creative imagination. In order to heal I learned there had to be a balance between work, rest, and play which I had never had in my life. Well during the seven years of my transformation, my body would take no other response but to be removed from society and rest and sleep all day and night. I had pushed it to the limit and it had to recover. My work was heavy, long, and intense each and every day of my transforming. I worked long hours to learn my beliefs and blockages that were controlling my life. So for having fun, which there wasn't much of, I used my imagination to create fictitious people in my closet. I could bring out these characters whenever I wanted them for company and fun. Hence in my book I have shared my descriptions of some of the men I created to have fun with and keep balance in my life. Maybe one day they will also be manifested along with my other invention ideas.

I discovered another great gift I had during this time. I had always wanted to do art but had never had any training or lessons even in school for it. I started water color painting and then was loaned a book on Mandalas. I discovered I could meditate and ask for the perfect healing symbols to heal something and the results "flowed" through my hands. I never knew what the pieces would look like until they were finished. Neither could I copy any of them if asked to. They are all very uniquely original. To this day, I have over one hundred that I have completed and continue to do them. I have successfully been able to do them for other people also.

The Mandalas were a huge healing tool for me during my transformation. The sacred geometry symbols and the colors have great healing ability on the brain. This healing occurs just by looking at the picture. I believe they help to retrain your brain. I hope to work my gifts even more and let my art help many others to heal.

I know now I had to have this clearing and healing in order to do the work I came here to do. I had chosen the hardest path, because I had ignored my body and its warning signs all my life. The Universe had to put me down flat, so I would listen and do what I needed to do. I am very hard headed. You can choose an easier quicker path of healing if you pay attention to your body, what it needs, and take action to help it.

Once during my first year I saw a patient who had obviously had the illness longer than I had, and I asked her how long she had been sick. She said oh I have been sick for five years and she went on to tell me that you never get well from environmental illness. She said you must learn to live with it as you can never heal from it. I remember so distinctly this conversation. When I heard her words I remember how they hit my body and how my body responded. Again, I remember all the details like it was in slow motion. My entire being froze immediately to shield against and not accept any of her energy, words, thoughts, or emotions that she was putting out toward me. I was not accepting any part of that. I knew I would heal totally and live a very normal life again and I am.

I believe that the environmental illness developed to help change the world. Most of the first diagnosed people that came down with it were Type A women nearing fifty. They were Warriors who had just lost their way. Now all ages and sexes are being diagnosed with it. It is an illness to teach us that all the energy fields interact together and healing only the physical body is not a complete healing. It also very clearly teaches us that taking care of a symptom is not the way to heal an illness. We must heal the emotions and mental and spiritual fields in order to have lasting total complete healing. We must find the root cause of the symptom and not just mask it in order to cure someone. This illness will help cause an integration of western and eastern medicine.

Okay, so with my belief system I am not the fastest manifester around but I am going to get there sooner than later. I am starting to catch on to how this is done. I wanted a crystal ball most of my life and finally manifested a beautiful one for $25.00 on Amazon with free shipping after a friend said just get one. I was playing victim to a $25 item that I didn't think I could have. Of course, I had not researched and thought it cost way more money than I had to spend on it. I preferred to make the victim statement of not having something I really wanted for many years, rather than trying to see if I could really have it.

I held that very crystal ball one morning stating my clear intent to write a book that would help the majority of people to awaken and live a joyful healthy life on the new moon of July 8, 2013. The new moon is when astrologers suggest you state and make your desires known to the Universe.

I stated to Mr. Wonder that I knew I was to write a book but could not get it started. He responded just sit down and write one page. That is how my book finally started. He was mirroring back to me (it is never about the other person, it is always about us) what I always say to others. Just Do It Already….What are you waiting for? Thanks to Nike I'd had a black button since the 8th grade with their motto….Just Do It. I also remembered numerous occurrences of late where my daily card pulled from the deck was "postponement".

So why not? I asked myself. I've known since early in my life I would be writing a book or books. Isn't it about time to do it? I have requested a much larger income with a lot less work hours……earn money while I sleep philosophy….(also learned from a friend). Write your book now! So I did start it and had a lot of postponing at times. But I did it.

I want to help you realize and live the dream you've always had without all the postponing. Just Do your Dream!

For many of you it may be buried and forgotten, only to be an uneasy restless feeling arising at times that you barely notice anymore. Some of you may feel it trying to push itself into action, but you always seem to push it back down. For others you may talk about it and have a "story" around why you will never be able to do it, citing many excuses of why it won't happen. You may have a "story" about how one day you will do it, but that day is always down the road and never appears. Doing your dream is always on the horizon of future tomorrows.

Then I identify the group that I call the extremes. Either they proclaim so many dreams they could never do them all and/or they don't even know what their dream is. The extremes always say their statement with over exaggerated faked emotional energy, or they state it with dead emotion which means stagnate to no emotional energy behind their statement. Their eyes always reveal their true story to me.

There is another group that states they are living their dream, but the careful observer can see that they are not telling their full truth. They try to make themselves believe they are, when in fact they are only living the belief of fake it until you make it. They have "settled" or "sold out" for something less than they really want, and they try to pretend it is wonderful and all they can ever have.

Another segment of people are speaking their truth about really doing their dream, and they are a rare group that is growing in number each and every day now. My dream is to help you join that group! The younger generations coming in are much more adapt at knowing and doing what they want, or at lease at making the changes to get what they want.

I want you eager to wake each morning, with the burning desire to start the day because it is so much fun and so fulfilling. Laughter is your first choice of business each and every day. It comes naturally and flows freely. You feel happy and carefree. You have good health and you feel energized. You have new and wonderful thoughts about your work and how you can serve people. You find your work satisfying and rewarding. Your work is your play and your play is your work. Your eyes dance and sparkle with the joy of your play work. You are successful beyond what you could have ever imagined.

Do Your Dream!

I can look into your eyes and know if you are doing your dream.

I want to help you overcome any or all of the following.

- You feel something good rising from the pit of your stomach that unsettles you, and you continue to push it back down.
- You have a "story" around why you will never be able to do what you want to do.
- You have a "story" about how one day you will do your dream. It always waits for you on the horizon of future tomorrows.

- You proclaim so many dreams that you could never do them all.
- You don't know what your dream really is.
- You fear being a failure or making a mistake, if you go for your dream.
- You have "settled and sold out" for less than what you want.
- You are living a pretend life and you feel it inside. You know there is more.
- You let everyone else advise and control your life.
- You are dead inside and feel trapped in your life due to responsibility, fear, guilt, etc.

I want this for you.

- Wake laughing and eager each morning to start the day and see what it holds.
- Your work is your play and your play is your work.
- You feel happy and carefree.
- You have a streak of being mischievous and playful.
- You are in the best health and you have lots of energy.
- You are successful beyond what you have ever imagined.
- You are confident, strong and ready to handle whatever comes your way.
- People are happy after they have been around you.
- You feel in love and you live in gratitude.
- You claim and speak your truth and power regardless of the opinions of others.

Which of these two descriptions do you want to live and be an example for others to see?

Children and others learn by what they see you do.

I want to help you realize and live the life you really want.

It's Time To Do Your Dream!

Be the Warrior you are!

It took me as a Warrior seven years to fully recover and feel like I was almost normal again, because I was so hard headed. I say almost because I really want to incorporate play into my work, without it devaluing it and taking away from the integrity and serious endeavor of it.

I have been called Tinker Bell, Earth Muffin, Playful One, Wild Woman, Too Optimistic, Science Fiction and other such names. I am playful and light hearted and as such I am going to go with my heart, even though it defies every business guideline and society rule that my brain believes exists.

As the Warrior I am, I now emerge from the dark jungle fog, sparkling with Light, coming forth to share what I have learned from all of my experiences, to work my gifts, and stand solid in my power as a Healer.

I am the playful one that inspires you to heal and be you!

.......It's Not.......

...........THE END...........

..........It's Our Beginning..........

Next book coming soon

Red Wine & Roses

A self-help book on how do I really learn to love myself.

www.kathydcarter.com

www.ingramcontent.com/pod-product-compliance
Lightning Source LLC
Chambersburg PA
CBHW070511090426
42735CB00012B/2739